SIGN REFERENCES
(signs used in the maps and diagrams)

Good footpath
(sufficiently distinct to be followed in mist)

Intermittent footpath
(difficult to follow in mist)

Route recommended
but no path
(if recommended one way only, arrow indicates direction)

Wall ◦◦◦◦◦◦◦◦◦◦◦◦   Broken wall ◦ ◦ ◦ ◦ ◦ ◦ ◦ ◦ ◦ ◦ ◦

Fence ++++++++++   Broken fence ıııııııııııııı

Marshy ground   Trees

Crags   Boulders

Stream or River
(arrow indicates direction of flow)

Waterfall   Bridge

Buildings   Unenclosed road

Contours (at 100' intervals)   1900 1800 1700

Summ   △

A PICTORIAL GUIDE
TO THE
LAKELAND FELLS
50TH ANNIVERSARY EDITION

being an illustrated account
of a study and exploration
of the mountains in the
English Lake District

by

A Wainwright

BOOK THREE
THE CENTRAL FELLS

Frances Lincoln Limited
4 Torriano Mews
Torriano Avenue
London NW5 2RZ
www.franceslincoln.com

Originally published by Henry Marsall, Kentmere, 1958

First published by Frances Lincoln 2003

50th Anniversary Edition with re-originated artwork
published by Frances Lincoln 2005

Printed and bound in Italy

A CIP catalogue record for this book
is available from the British Library.

ISBN 978 0 7112 2456 8

9 8 7 6 5 4 3

50TH ANNIVERSARY EDITION
PUBLISHED BY
FRANCES LINCOLN, LONDON

THE PICTORIAL GUIDES

PUBLISHER'S NOTE

This 50th Anniversary edition of the Pictorial Guides to the Lakeland Fells is newly reproduced from the handwritten pages created in the 1950s and 1960s by A. Wainwright. The descriptions of the walks were correct, to the best of the author's knowledge, at the time of first publication and they are reproduced here without amendment. However, footpaths, cairns and other waymarks described here are no longer all as they were fifty years ago and walkers are advised to check with an up-to-date map when planning a walk.

Fellwalking has increased dramatically since the Pictorial Guides were first published. Some popular routes have become eroded, making good footwear and great care all the more necessary for walkers. The vital points about fellwalking, as A. Wainwright himself wrote on many occasions, are to use common sense and to remember to watch where you are putting your feet.

A programme of revision of the Pictorial Guides is under way and revised editions of each of them will be published over the next few years.

BOOK THREE
is dedicated to
those eager explorers of the fells

THE DOGS OF LAKELAND

willing workers and faithful friends,
and an essential part of Lakeland life

INTRODUCTION

Classification and Definition

Any division of the Lakeland fells into geographical districts must necessarily be arbitrary, just as the location of the outer boundaries of Lakeland must always be a matter of opinion. Any attempt to define internal or external boundaries is certain to invite criticism, and he who takes it upon himself to say where Lakeland starts and finishes, or, for example, where the Central Fells merge into the Southern Fells and *which* fells are the Central Fells and which the Southern and *why* they need be so classified, must not expect his pronouncements to be generally accepted.

Yet for present purposes some plan of classification and definition must be used. County and parochial boundaries are no help, nor is the recently-defined area of the Lakeland National Park, for this book is concerned only with the high ground.

First, the external boundaries. Straight lines linking the extremities of the outlying lakes enclose all the higher fells very conveniently. There are a few fells of lesser height to the north and east, however, that are typically Lakeland in character and cannot properly be omitted : these are brought in, somewhat untidily, by extending the lines in those areas. Thus :

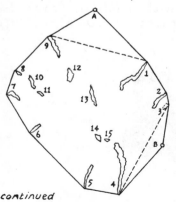

1 : *Ullswater*
2 : *Hawes Water*
3 : proposed *Swindale Resr*
4 : *Windermere*
5 : *Coniston Water*
6 : *Wast Water*
7 : *Ennerdale Water*
8 : *Loweswater*
9 : *Bassenthwaite Lake*
10 : *Crummock Water*
11 : *Buttermere*
12 : *Derwent Water*
13 : *Thirlmere*
14 : *Grasmere*
15 : *Rydal Water*
A : *Caldbeck*
B : *Longsleddale (church)*

continued

Classification and Definition

continued

        The complete Guide is planned to include all the fells in the area enclosed by the straight lines of the diagram. This is an undertaking quite beyond the compass of a single volume, and it is necessary, therefore, to divide the area into convenient sections, making the fullest use of natural boundaries (lakes, valleys and low passes) so that each district is, as far as possible, self-contained and independent of the rest.

This division gives seven areas, each with a well-defined group of fells, and each will be the subject of a separate volume

1 : The Eastern Fells
2 : The Far Eastern Fells
3 : The Central Fells
4 : The Southern Fells
5 : The Northern Fells
6 : The North-western Fells
7 : The Western Fells

Notes on the Illustrations

THE MAPS.................Many excellent books have been written about Lakeland, but the best literature of all for the walker is that published by the Director General of Ordnance Survey, the 1" map for companionship and guidance on expeditions, the 2½" map for exploration both on the fells and by the fireside. These admirable maps are remarkably accurate topographically but there is a crying need for a revision of the paths on the hills: several walkers' tracks that have come into use during the past few decades, some of them now broad highways, are not shown at all; other paths still shown on the maps have fallen into neglect and can no longer be traced on the ground.

The popular Bartholomew 1" map is a beautiful picture, fit for a frame, but this too is unreliable for paths; indeed here the defect is much more serious, for routes are indicated where no paths ever existed, nor ever could — the cartographer has preferred to take precipices in his stride rather than deflect his graceful curves over easy ground.

Hence the justification for the maps in this book: they have the one merit (of importance to walkers) of being dependable as regards delineation of *paths*. They are intended as supplements to the Ordnance Survey maps, certainly not as substitutes.

THE VIEWS................Various devices have been used to illustrate the views from the summits of the fells. The full panorama in the form of an outline drawing is most satisfactory generally, and this method has been adopted for the main viewpoints.

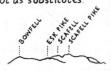

THE DIAGRAMS OF ASCENTS..................The routes of ascent of the higher fells are depicted by diagrams that do not pretend to strict accuracy: they are neither plans nor elevations; in fact there is deliberate distortion in order to show detail clearly: usually they are represented as viewed from imaginary 'space-stations.' But it is hoped they will be useful and interesting.

THE DRAWINGS.......The drawings at least are honest attempts to reproduce what the eye sees: they illustrate features of interest and also serve the dual purpose of breaking up the text and balancing the layout of the pages, and of filling up awkward blank spaces, like this:

Thirlmere

THE
CENTRAL
FELLS

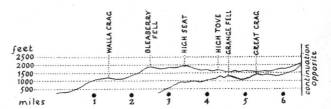

Similar in plan to the Eastern and the Far Eastern fells, the high ground of the central area of Lakeland is based on a north-south axis. Deep valleys isolate the mass from the surrounding fells, there being a link with other mountainous terrain only at the Stake Pass. The north-south axis in its lower extremity twists eastwards in this case, however, the area assuming the shape of a jackboot, with Ambleside at the toe, Stake Pass forming the heel's curve, and the leg extending north, between the valleys of Borrowdale and Thirlmere, to the River Greta and Keswick.

The central part of mountainous country might generally be expected to contain the highest peaks, but that is not so here, for the watershed is overtopped on all sides by summits of greater elevation, and only at one point, High Raise, is an altitude of 2500' reached. Nevertheless the central mass is not insignificant and indeed within its boundaries is one particular concentration of mountains, crowded into small space, that, for popular appeal and scenic attractiveness, ranks second to none : the Langdale Pikes.

The best part of the central area for fellwalkers is that south of the Grasmere-Borrowdale crossing via Greenup, for, in addition to the Pikes, the lesser heights declining to the rivers Rothay and Brathay are very colourful and interesting, with crags everywhere, while the views from them include a rich array of lovely lakes.

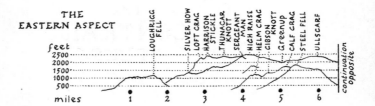

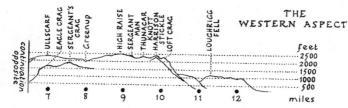

North of Greenup the terrain is of different character, the main watershed widening and levelling out to such an extent that the rain falling upon it can disperse but slowly; consequently there are many swamps, the worst in Lakeland, where walkers seldom venture. It is a sufficient commentary that in the course of the eight miles from Greenup to Rakefoot this ridge, although in the very heart of the district, is crossed by two footpaths only. But the shortcomings of the ridge in this section are amply compensated by the charm and beauty of the foothills, particularly overlooking Borrowdale: here the immediate surroundings and the distant views are alike supremely lovely. On the Thirlmere side, too, there is a fascination in the silent forests and gaunt crags above the dark waters of the lake.

The area south of Greenup, the fells west of Grasmere, and the Borrowdale flank are all exceedingly favoured by walkers (a circumstance that has led to the provision of much excellent accommodation in the nearby valleys) and are admirably suitable for the holiday-maker whose preference is not so much for the longer excursions and rougher walking demanded by the higher mountains but rather for easier rambles on fells of lesser altitude yet sufficiently high and distinctive to afford that feeling, so wonderfully satisfying, of 'being on the tops'.

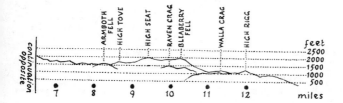

THE CENTRAL FELLS

Natural Boundaries

Fells, in order of altitude:

1 : HIGH RAISE
2 : SERGEANT MAN
3 : HARRISON STICKLE
4 : ULLSCARF
5 : THUNACAR KNOTT
6 : PIKE O' STICKLE
7 : PAVEY ARK
8 : LOFT CRAG
9 : HIGH SEAT
10 : BLEABERRY FELL
11 : SERGEANT'S CRAG
12 : STEEL FELL
13 : TARN CRAG
14 : BLEA RIGG
15 : CALF CRAG
16 : HIGH TOVE
17 : EAGLE CRAG
18 : ARMBOTH FELL
19 : RAVEN CRAG
20 : GREAT CRAG
21 : GIBSON KNOTT
22 : GRANGE FELL
23 : HELM CRAG
24 : SILVER HOW
25 : WALLA CRAG
26 : HIGH RIGG
27 : LOUGHRIGG FELL

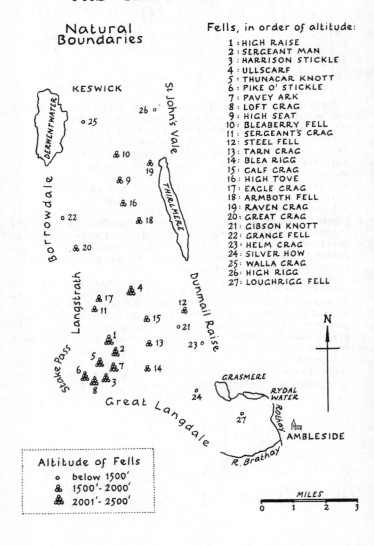

Altitude of Fells

- o   below 1500'
- &   1500'- 2000'
- && 2001'- 2500'

THE CENTRAL FELLS

in the order of
their appearance
in this book

Reference to map opposite

2001'-2500'	1500'-2000'	below 1500'		Altitude in feet
	18		ARMBOTH FELL	1570
	10		BLEABERRY FELL	1932
	14		BLEA RIGG	1776
	15		CALF CRAG	1762
	17		EAGLE CRAG	1650
		21	GIBSON KNOTT	1379
		22	GRANGE FELL	1363
	20		GREAT CRAG	1500
3			HARRISON STICKLE	2403
		23	HELM CRAG	1299
1			HIGH RAISE	2500
		26	HIGH RIGG	1163
	9		HIGH SEAT	1995
	16		HIGH TOVE	1665
8			LOFT CRAG	2270
		27	LOUGHRIGG FELL	1101
7			PAVEY ARK	2288
6			PIKE O' STICKLE	2323
	19		RAVEN CRAG	1520
2			SERGEANT MAN	2414
	11		SERGEANT'S CRAG	1873
		24	SILVER HOW	1292
	12		STEEL FELL	1811
	13		TARN CRAG	1801
5			THUNACAR KNOTT	2351
4			ULLSCARF	2370
		25	WALLA CRAG	1234
8	12	7		
27				

Each fell is the subject
of a separate chapter

Armboth Fell

from Fisher Crag

Armboth Fell has probably as good a claim as any to be regarded as the most centrally situated fell in Lakeland, for straight lines drawn between the northern and southern boundaries, and between the eastern and western, would bisect hereabouts. (Since these boundaries are arbitrary, however, individual opinion will differ on this point).

Peak-baggers and record-chasers may have cause to visit the summit, but other walkers may justifiably consider its ascent a waste of precious time and energy when so many more rewarding climbs are available, for the flat desolate top is little better than a quagmire, a tangle of swamp and heather and mosses, as is much of the surrounding territory. It can be said of very few fells that they are not really worth climbing; Armboth Fell is one of the few.

The fell lies to the east of the central ridge, and the rain that falls upon it either elects to stay there for ever or drains slowly away towards Thirlmere, hurrying only down the steep afforested slopes immediately flanking the reservoir. Such scenic beauty as Armboth Fell has to offer is wholly concentrated in this wooded fringe above Thirlmere, where there are splendid crags and waterfalls, of which Fisher Crag and Launchy Gill are outstanding. The dark forests conceal the dying traces of a lost civilisation, lost not so very long ago.

HIGH SEAT ▲
Armboth
▲ HIGH TOVE
• Watendlath
▲ ARMBOTH FELL
Wythburn

▲ ULLSCARF

MILES
0   1   2   3

ASCENT FROM THIRLMERE

Walkers of a contrary turn of mind will summarily reject the advice to leave Armboth Fell alone and may indeed be strengthened in their determination to climb it; nor are they likely to be deterred by the many TRESPASSERS WILL BE PROSECUTED notices that Manchester Corporation have sprinkled about the landscape. They would be further outraged if, having paid 12s 6d for this book, they found it did not cater for their idiosyncrasies by offering some details of routes of ascent. Here then are four routes, all starting from the road along the west shore of Thirlmere:

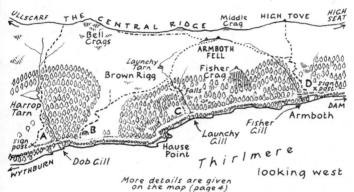

More details are given on the map (page 4)

A : Public footpath. A well-known path, going on to Watendlath. For Armboth Fell leave it at the ridge by a poor track that keeps right of the fence. This route is very wet underfoot throughout: the path in the Harrop Tarn plantations is abominably muddy and even almost impassable in places, for which state of affairs forestry operations are largely to blame.

B : North of Dobgill Bridge a wide section of fellside is unplanted, and a good dry path climbs it. For Armboth Fell leave the path at the top wall and bear right above the plantations, crossing Launchy Gill. This is not a right of way, but until the responsible authorities effect some repairs to the Harrop Tarn footpath trespass here should be forgiven.

C : An old signboard on the roadside at the foot of Launchy Gill now bears no message but in its heyday probably announced the usual threats. An intermittent track on the left (south) bank leads to a desperate struggle with massed conifers before the fell is reached. After rain, the waterfalls provide a magnificent spectacle.

D : Public footpath (to Watendlath). At the top wall bear left and cross and follow up Fisher Gill. Marshy patches.

A balanced boulder, 12 feet high, alongside the footpath from Armboth

MAP

Although the boundaries of Armboth Fell are strictly defined by Fisher Gill and Launchy Gill, this map includes also much indefinite country southwards to Harrop Tarn and westwards to Bleatarn Gill, some of it reaching a greater elevation than Armboth Fell but having no recognised summits.

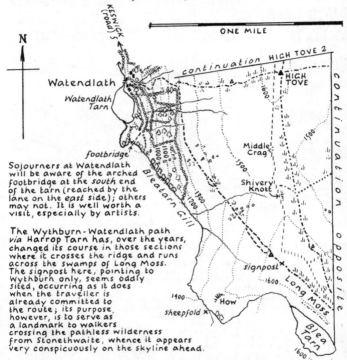

Sojourners at Watendlath will be aware of the arched footbridge at the *south* end of the tarn (reached by the lane on the *east* side); others may not. It is well worth a visit, especially by artists.

The Wythburn–Watendlath path *via* Harrop Tarn has, over the years, changed its course in those sections where it crosses the ridge and runs across the swamps of Long Moss. The signpost here, pointing to Wythburn only, seems oddly sited, occurring as it does when the traveller is already committed to the route; its purpose, however, is to serve as a landmark to walkers crossing the pathless wilderness from Stonethwaite, whence it appears very conspicuously on the skyline ahead.

Hidden away in the gloom of the Thirlmere plantations are many reminders of community life here before Manchester condemned the area to a slow death and an everlasting silence. Ruined farmsteads and shepherds' huts, overgrown cart-roads, and crumbling allotment and intake walls, deprived of sunlight, have become spectral ghosts, green with moss, in the depths of the forest; the cairns erected to mark the Harrop Tarn path when it traversed an open fellside still stand, heavily overshadowed by trees. The west side of Thirlmere had its illicit whisky distilleries and cockpits, too, and altogether a very interesting history. Now all is buried beneath a green shroud.

MAP

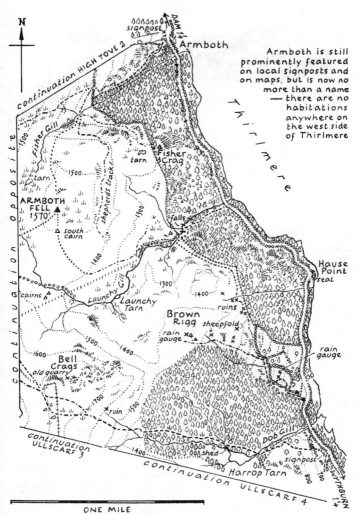

N

signpost
Armboth

continuation HIGH TOVE 2

Armboth is still
prominently featured
on local signposts and
on maps, but is now no
more than a name
— there are no
habitations
anywhere on the
west side
of Thirlmere

Thirlmere

Fisher Gill

tarn

Fisher
Crag

1500

tarn

shepherds track

falls

ARMBOTH
FELL 1570

south
cairn

continuation opposite

1400

1300

Hause
Point
seat

cairns

Launchy Gill

Launchy
Tarn

1300

ruins

Brown
Rigg

sheepfold

1400

rain
gauge

rain
gauge

1500

1400

Bell
Crags
old quarry

1600

1700

ruin

1500

Dob Gill

continuation
ULLSCARF 3

shed

signpost

800

700

WYTHBURN 1¼

1400

continuation ULLSCARF 4

Harrop Tarn

ONE MILE

THE SUMMIT

A few stones heaped together on a rocky mound indicate the highest point although another prominence east of north would seem to have an equal claim to that distinction. The top of the fell is a wide plateau of heather and bog, and the cairn is not easy to locate even in clear weather, especially if approached from the east.

A furlong south of the summit-cairn, at a lower elevation, is a well-built shepherd's cairn on a rock.

THE VIEW

The Helvellyn range dominates the scene, but the best features are westwards, overtopping the central ridge.

Principal Fells

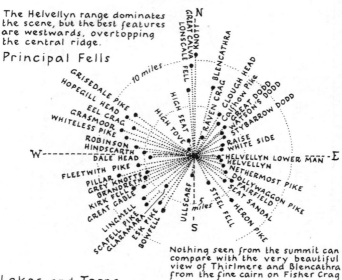

Nothing seen from the summit can compare with the very beautiful view of Thirlmere and Blencathra from the fine cairn on Fisher Crag

Lakes and Tarns

None, except a few nameless puddles in the vicinity.

RIDGE ROUTES

To HIGH TOVE, 1665':
1 mile : W. then N
Depression at 1475'
200 feet of ascent
Dreariness and desolation
The tempting beeline cannot be done because of bog. Aim west for the ridge-path, such as it is.

To ULLSCARF, 2370':
3 miles : SW, then S, SW and S
Sundry depressions, all marshy
950 feet of ascent
Squelch, squelch, squelch all the way.
A wet and weary trudge along the swampiest ridge in the district. A path may be joined 200 yards short of Shivery Knott (indistinct just here)

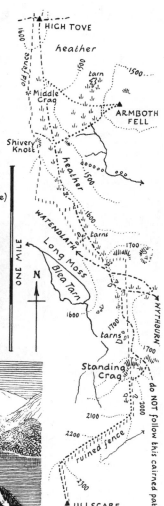

Waterfalls in Launchy Gill

View from Fisher Crag
VISITORS HERE WILL BE PROSECUTED

Bleaberry Fell

1932'

from Ashness Wood

• Keswick

WALLA   • Dale
CRAG ▲   Bottom

BLEABERRY
     ▲ FELL

• Lodore
    ▲ HIGH SEAT

MILES

0   1   2   3

The Shoulthwaite Crags

Goat Crags →

Iron Crag ↓

NATURAL FEATURES

Bleaberry Fell terminates the central ridge to the north in much the same manner as Clough Head and Loadpot Hill terminate the parallel Helvellyn and High Street ridges on the eastern side of the district, and it is similar in formation, appearing as a lofty rounded dome overlooking the Keswick to Penrith gap. Unlike the eastern ridges, however, which give good walking throughout over a series of interesting summits, the greater part of the central ridge is marshy and the summits dreary (north of Greenup): unsuitable territory for fell-walking. But Bleaberry Fell is a magnificent exception: it is a superb viewpoint, ideally situated for a long and lazy contemplation of a beautiful panorama. What is more, and here it scores heavily over other fells along the ridge, it can be climbed dryshod and the short springy heather of the top is a joy to tread.

Borrowdale on the west side, and the Naddle and Shoulthwaite valleys eastwards, are the boundaries, both flanks being buttressed by steep crags, notably Iron Crag and Goat Crags above Shoulthwaite and the better-known Falcon Crag above Derwentwater.

From the summit a lower and less definite ridge continues over Dodd Crag and Pike before coming down to the pastures of Rakefoot and then sloping gently to the Vale of Keswick accompanied by the pleasant Brockle Beck, the fell's main stream.

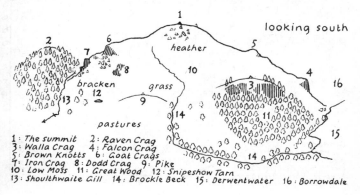

looking south

1: The summit   2: Raven Crag
3: Walla Crag   4: Falcon Crag
5: Brown Knotts   6: Goat Crags
7: Iron Crag   8: Dodd Crag   9: Pike
10: Low Moss   11: Great Wood   12: Snipeshow Tarn
13: Shoulthwaite Gill   14: Brockle Beck   15: Derwentwater   16: Borrowdale

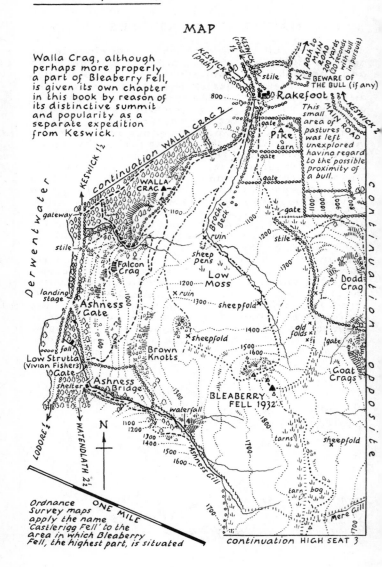

MAP

Walla Crag, although
perhaps more properly
a part of Bleaberry Fell,
is given its own chapter
in this book by reason of
its distinctive summit
and popularity as a
separate expedition
from Keswick.

BEWARE OF
THE BULL (if any)

Rakefoot

This small
area of
pastures
was left
unexplored
having regard
to the possible
proximity of
a bull

WALLA CRAG 2

Derwentwater

WALLA CRAG

Brockle Beck

Falcon Crag

Low Moss

Dodd Crag

landing stage

Ashness Gate

ruin

sheep pens

sheepfold

old folds

Low Strutta
(Vivian Fishers)
Gate

Ashness Bridge

shelter

Brown Knotts

sheepfold

Goat Crags

waterfall

BLEABERRY FELL 1932

N

LODORE ½

WATENDLATH 2½

Ashness Gill

tarns

sheepfold

ONE MILE

Ordnance
Survey maps
apply the name
'Castlerigg Fell' to the
area in which Bleaberry
Fell, the highest part, is situated

tarn-bog

Mere Gill

continuation HIGH SEAT 3

ASCENT FROM THE BORROWDALE ROAD
1650 feet of ascent : 1¼ miles

This is a beautiful climb, rough in places, as far as the waterfalls; thereafter the trudge across the moor is dreary. The views are superb. *Don't forget the camera.*

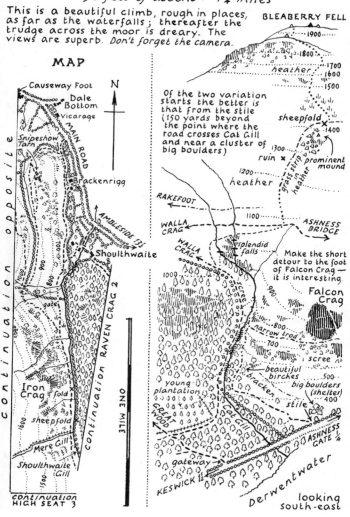

BLEABERRY FELL

MAP

Of the two variation starts the better is that from the stile (150 yards beyond the point where the road crosses Cat Gill and near a cluster of big boulders)

Make the short detour to the foot of Falcon Crag — it is interesting

Causeway Foot
Dale Bottom
Vicarage
Snipeshow Tarn
Brackenrigg
AMBLESIDE 13½
Shoulthwaite
gate
Iron Crag
fold
sheepfold
Mere Gill
Shoulthwaite Gill

MAIN ROAD
N

continuation opposite
continuation RAVEN CRAG 2
ONE MILE
continuation HIGH SEAT 3

1900
1800
heather
1700
1600
1500
sheepfold
1400
1300
ruin ×
prominent mound
grass strip
heather
1200
heather
RAKEFOOT
WALLA CRAG
1100
ASHNESS BRIDGE
WALLA CRAG
splendid falls
Falcon Crag
1000
900
800
narrow trod
700
scree
beautiful birches
bracken
500
big boulders (shelter)
400
stile
young plantation
GREAT WOOD
Cat Gill
ASHNESS GATE ¼
gateway
KESWICK 1½
Derwentwater

looking south-east

ASCENT FROM KESWICK
1650 feet of ascent : 3½ miles

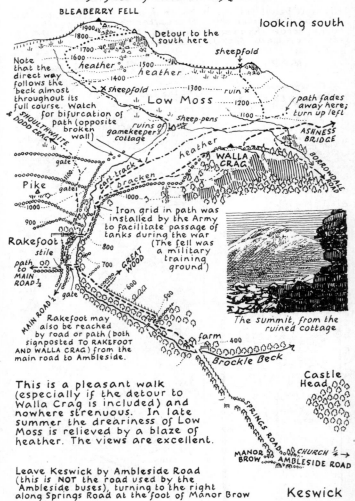

BLEABERRY FELL

looking south

1900
1800
Detour to the south here
1700
sheepfold
1600
heather
1500
Note that the direct way follows the beck almost throughout its full course. Watch for bifurcation of path (opposite broken wall)
1400
heather
1300
ruin
1200
path fades away here; turn up left
1100

SHOULTHWAITE DODD CRAG

sheepfold

Low Moss

ASHNESS BRIDGE

ruins of gamekeeper's cottage

sheep-pens

heather

WALLA CRAG

BORROWDALE ROAD

gate

cart-track

bracken

Pike

gate

1000

Iron grid in path was installed by the Army to facilitate passage of tanks during the war (The fell was a military training ground)

900

Rakefoot

stile

800

GREAT WOOD

700

path to MAIN ROAD ¼

600

MAIN ROAD 2

gate

The summit, from the ruined cottage

Rakefoot may also be reached by road or path (both signposted TO RAKEFOOT AND WALLA CRAG) from the main road to Ambleside.

farm

400

Brockle Beck

Castle Head

This is a pleasant walk (especially if the detour to Walla Crag is included) and nowhere strenuous. In late summer the dreariness of Low Moss is relieved by a blaze of heather. The views are excellent.

SPRINGS ROAD

Leave Keswick by Ambleside Road (this is NOT the road used by the Ambleside buses), turning to the right along Springs Road at the foot of Manor Brow

MANOR BROW

CHURCH ½

AMBLESIDE ROAD

Keswick

ASCENT FROM DALE BOTTOM
1600 feet of ascent : 3 miles (5½ from Keswick)

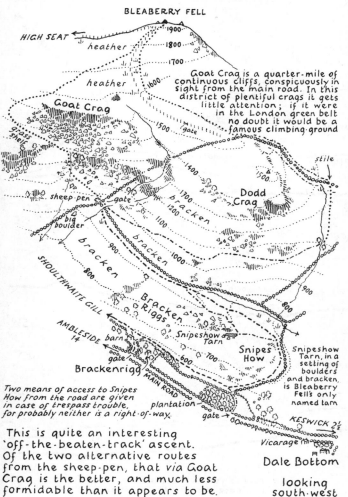

BLEABERRY FELL

HIGH SEAT

heather

1900
1800
1700
1600

heather

Goat Crag

Goat Crag is a quarter-mile of continuous cliffs, conspicuously in sight from the main road. In this district of plentiful crags it gets little attention; if it were in the London green belt no doubt it would be a famous climbing-ground

1500
gate

grass shelf

stile

1400

1500

Dodd Crag

sheep pen
gate

big boulder

1300
bracken
1200

1100

bracken

1000

900
bracken

bracken

800
SHOULTHWAITE GILL

900

800

Bracken Riggs

Snipeshow Tarn

Snipes How

Snipeshow Tarn, in a setting of boulders and bracken, is Bleaberry Fell's only named tarn

AMBLESIDE 14

barn
gate

Brackenrigg

600
MAIN ROAD

700

Two means of access to Snipes How from the road are given in case of trespass trouble, for probably neither is a right-of-way.

plantation

gate

KESWICK 2½

Vicarage

Dale Bottom

looking south-west

This is quite an interesting 'off-the-beaten-track' ascent. Of the two alternative routes from the sheep-pen, that *via* Goat Crag is the better, and much less formidable than it appears to be.

THE VIEW

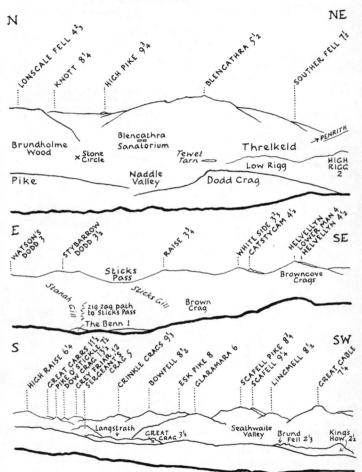

The figures following the names of fells
indicate distances in miles

THE VIEW

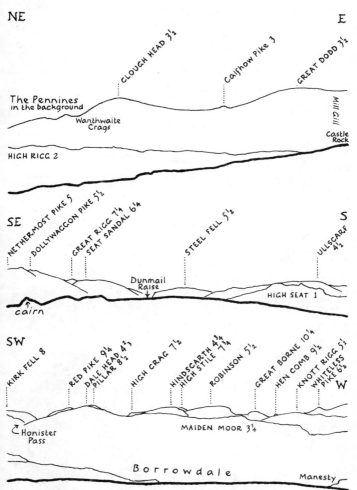

NE

CLOUGH HEAD 3½   Calfhow Pike 3   GREAT DODD 3½

E

The Pennines
in the background

Wanthwaite Crags   Mill Gill

Castle Rock

HIGH RIGG 2

SE

NETHERMOST PIKE 5
DOLLYWAGGON PIKE 5½
GREAT RIGG 7¼
SEAT SANDAL 6¼

STEEL FELL 5½

ULLSCARF 4½

S

Dunmail Raise

cairn

HIGH SEAT 1

SW

KIRK FELL 8

RED PIKE 9¼
DALE HEAD 4²/₃
PILLAR 8½

HIGH CRAG 7½

HINDSCARTH 4¾
HIGH STILE 7¼

ROBINSON 5½

GREAT BORNE 10¼
HEN COMB 9½
KNOTT RIGG 5½
WHITELESS PIKE 6½

W

Honister Pass

MAIDEN MOOR 3¼

Borrowdale

Manesty

The thick line marks the visible boundaries
of the summit-plateau

continued

THE VIEW

continued

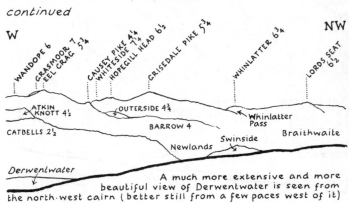

W

WANDOPE 6
GRASMOOR 7
EEL CRAG 5¾
CAUSEY PIKE 4¼
WHITESIDE 7¼
HOPEGILL HEAD 6½
GRISEDALE PIKE 5¾
WHINLATTER 6¾
LORDS SEAT 6½

NW

ATKIN KNOTT 4½
OUTERSIDE 4¾
Whinlatter Pass

CATBELLS 2½
BARROW 4
Braithwaite

Newlands
Swinside

Derwentwater

A much more extensive and more beautiful view of Derwentwater is seen from the north-west cairn (better still from a few paces west of it)

THE SUMMIT

A carpet of short sweet heather makes the top a beautiful place, although there is nothing exciting about it other than the panorama, which is first-class. Three big cairns indicate viewpoints, while an insignificant fourth shows the way to High Seat in mist.

DESCENTS: Bearing in mind a line of low crags fringing the top to the north, there should not be any difficulty in descending to Keswick via Rakefoot, but ways down to the Borrowdale Road and Shoulthwaite need care even in clear weather. *In mist*, it is not advisable to try to get down to Shoulthwaite: the crags on this route are a dangerous trap.

YARDS
0   100

N

A
B
1700
heather
1800
1900
C
D

A: to Walla Crag and Borrowdale
B: to Keswick
C: to Shoulthwaite
D: to High Seat

Falcon Crag

THE VIEW

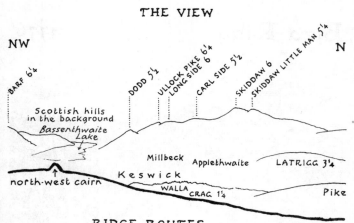

NW

N

BARF 6¼

DODD 5½

ULLOCK PIKE 6¼
LONG SIDE 6

CARL SIDE 5½

SKIDDAW 6
SKIDDAW LITTLE MAN 5¼

Scottish hills
in the background
*Bassenthwaite
Lake*

Millbeck   Applethwaite   LATRIGG 3¼

Keswick

north-west cairn

WALLA CRAG 1¼

Pike

RIDGE ROUTES

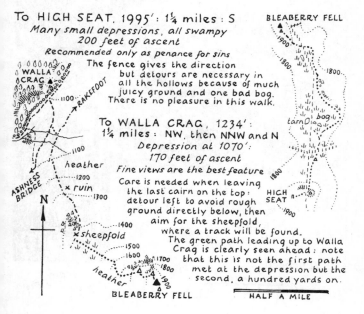

To **HIGH SEAT**, 1995′ : 1¼ miles : S
*Many small depressions, all swampy
200 feet of ascent
Recommended only as penance for sins*
The fence gives the direction
but detours are necessary in
all the hollows because of much
juicy ground and one bad bog.
There is no pleasure in this walk.

BLEABERRY FELL

1900

1800

1800

bog

tarn

1800

HIGH
SEAT

1900

To **WALLA CRAG**, 1234′ :
1¼ miles : NW, then NNW and N
*Depression at 1070′ :
170 feet of ascent
Fine views are the best feature*
Care is needed when leaving
the last cairn on the top :
detour left to avoid rough
ground directly below, then
aim for the sheepfold,
where a track will be found.
The green path leading up to Walla
Crag is clearly seen ahead : note
that this is not the first path
met at the depression but the
second, a hundred yards on.

WALLA
CRAG

RAKEFOOT

1100

1100

ASHNESS
BRIDGE

heather

1200

× ruin
1300

N

1400

× sheepfold

1500

1600

1700

1800

heather

1900

BLEABERRY FELL

HALF A MILE

Blea Rigg

1776'

HIGH RAISE
▲
BLEA RIGG
▲
Grasmere
●
Dungeon Ghyll
●
Ambleside
●

MILES
0 1 2 3 4

from
Greathead Crag

NATURAL FEATURES

The intricate and erratic ridge or shoulder that comes down from High Raise and, after a journey of several miles, expends itself at the meeting-place of the Rothay and Brathay rivers, is broad (a mile or more in places) and undulating (its descent being interrupted by a score of separate summits—many of them nameless). Hardly anywhere can it properly be described as a ridge for its features are akin to those of an upland plateau, but at one point a mild steepening of the sides and a comparative narrowness of the crest do confer a certain boldness of character. This place is Blea Rigg, which appears as a peaked top only when seen from lower down the shoulder. A long wall of crag overlooking Easedale Tarn is the great feature here; the opposite flank, falling to Great Langdale, is less impressive although on this side too there are considerable outcrops and faces of rock, notably along the course of White Gill. The slopes of Blea Rigg come down to Stickle Tarn on the one side and Easedale Tarn on the other, and the main mass of the fell may be said to lie between, but in this chapter, for convenience, will be included also the less definite adjoining part of the shoulder south-east to the point where a link is established with Silver How.

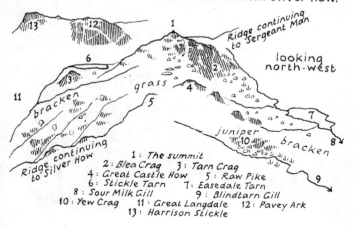

looking
north-west

Ridge continuing to Sergeant Man

Ridge continuing to Silver How

1 : The summit
2 : Blea Crag   3 : Tarn Crag
4 : Great Castle How   5 : Raw Pike
6 : Stickle Tarn   7 : Easedale Tarn
8 : Sour Milk Gill   9 : Blindtarn Gill
10 : Yew Crag   11 : Great Langdale   12 : Pavey Ark
13 : Harrison Stickle

MAP

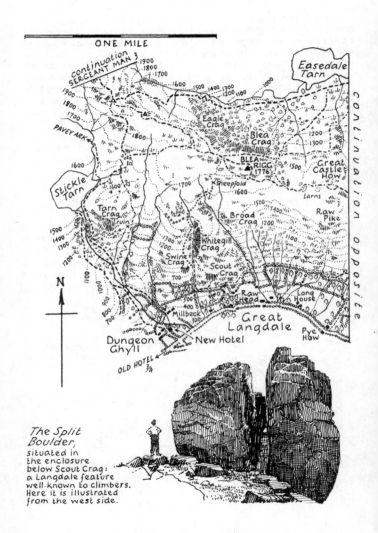

ONE MILE

Continuation
SERGEANT MAN 3

1900
1800
1700
1900
1800
1700

PAVEY ARK

1800

1600

Stickle
Tarn

1600

Tarn
Crag
ruin

1500
1490
1300
1200

1100
1000
800
700

N

1900
1800
1700
1600
1500 1400 1300 1200 1100 1000

Eagle
Crag

Blea
Crag

1200
1300

BLEA
RIGG
1776

1500

Great
Castle
How

Sheepfold
1600

tarns

1700

1400
1200

Broad
Crag

Raw
Pike

Whitegill
Crag

1200

1100

Swine
Crag

700

Scout
Crag

500
400
300

Millbeck

Raw
Head

Long
House

Great
Langdale

Pye
How

Dungeon
Ghyll

New Hotel

OLD HOTEL ¾

Easedale
Tarn

continuation opposite

*The Split
Boulder,*
situated in
the enclosure
below Scout Crag:
a Langdale feature
well-known to climbers.
Here it is illustrated
from the west side.

MAP

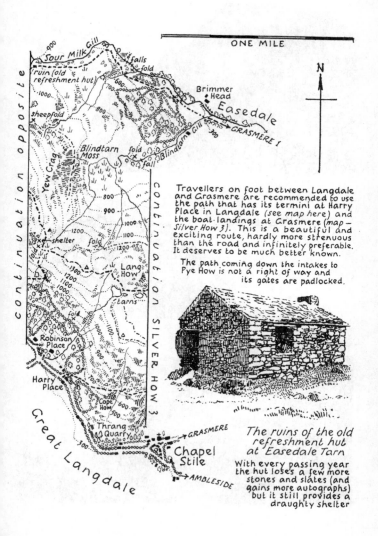

ONE MILE

N

Sour Milk Gill
falls
fold
ruin (old refreshment hut)
Brimmer Head
Easedale
GRASMERE 1
sheepfold
Blindtarn Moss
fold
fall
Blindtarn Gill
Yew Crag
shelter
fold
Lang How
tarns
Robinson Place
Harry Place
Copt How
Thrang Quarry
GRASMERE
Chapel Stile
AMBLESIDE
Great Langdale

continuation opposite

continuation SILVER HOW 3

Travellers on foot between Langdale and Grasmere are recommended to use the path that has its termini at Harry Place in Langdale (see map here) and the boat-landings at Grasmere (map — Silver How 3). This is a beautiful and exciting route, hardly more strenuous than the road and infinitely preferable. It deserves to be much better known.

The path coming down the intakes to Pye How is not a right of way and its gates are padlocked.

The ruins of the old refreshment hut at Easedale Tarn

With every passing year the hut loses a few more stones and slates (and gains more autographs) but it still provides a draughty shelter

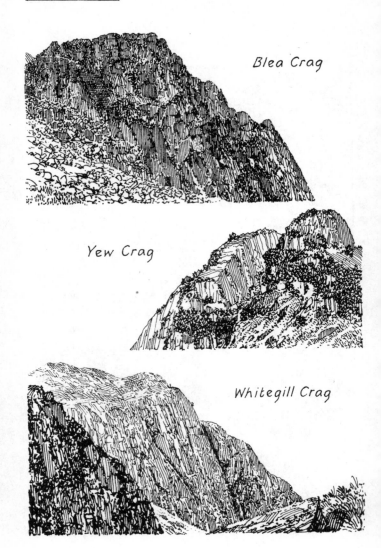

Blea Crag

Yew Crag

Whitegill Crag

ASCENT FROM GRASMERE
1600 feet of ascent : 3½ miles

SILVER HOW
BLEA RIGG
SERGEANT MAN →

Great Castle How
Blea Crag
Looking How

Here, either turn right up a grassy rake (cairns; steep) or go ahead to join ridge path near a perched boulder on a crag.

Eagle Crag

grass

1800
1700
1600

Belles Knott
waterslide

old tarn bed
bracken

hillock bracken

big boulder

slopes of TARN CRAG

old stone hut

← GRASMERE

Easedale Tarn

sheepfold

1500
1400
1300
1200
1100
1000
900

looking south-west

Instead of following the usual boggy path alongside the tarn and its main feeder to gain the ridge beyond the summit (this is a favourite way to Dungeon Ghyll) try one of the two direct routes illustrated: the first, from behind the hut, starts promisingly and finishes well but the intermediate section is swampy and dull; the second, with an indistinct start, is the better and it has the virtue (unique hereabouts) of being reasonably dry underfoot. Incidentally, apart from being a quick way to the top of Blea Rigg, this second route provides a direct link between Easedale and Stickle Tarns; a turn left from the main path 200 yards after crossing the first beck beyond the hut soon brings the track into sight as it skirts a small hillock (moraine) on the left side.

The direct routes illustrated are alternatives to the more popular approach along the Silver How ridge: they are especially useful if it is wished to 'save' the ridge for the return to Grasmere, the better way to walk it.

ASCENT FROM DUNGEON GHYLL (via TARN CRAG)
1550 feet of ascent · 2 miles from the New Hotel

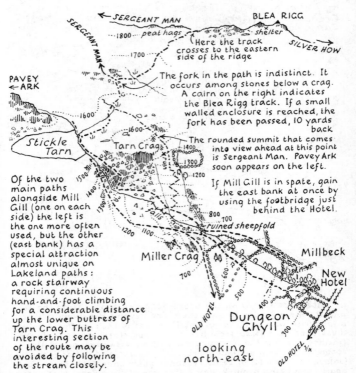

SERGEANT MAN

BLEA RIGG

SERGEANT MAN

PAVEY ARK

1800 peat hags

shelter

SILVER HOW

Here the track crosses to the eastern side of the ridge

1700

The fork in the path is indistinct. It occurs among stones below a crag. A cairn on the right indicates the Blea Rigg track. If a small walled enclosure is reached, the fork has been passed, 10 yards back

1600

Stickle Tarn

Tarn Crag

1600

1400

1300

1200

The rounded summit that comes into view ahead at this point is Sergeant Man. Pavey Ark soon appears on the left.

If Mill Gill is in spate, gain the east bank at once by using the footbridge just behind the Hotel.

Of the two main paths alongside Mill Gill (one on each side) the left is the one more often used, but the other (east bank) has a special attraction almost unique on Lakeland paths: a rock stairway requiring continuous hand-and-foot climbing for a considerable distance up the lower buttress of Tarn Crag. This interesting section of the route may be avoided by following the stream closely.

1500 1400 1300 1200 1100

800 700 ruined sheepfold

Miller Crag

Millbeck

New Hotel

1000

OLD HOTEL

700 600 500

Dungeon Ghyll

looking north-east

OLD HOTEL 1/4

Try the zig-zag alternative. This is the original path, well-engineered, and its grass is a pleasant relief from the stony tracks by the gill. Its start is easily passed unnoticed, the point of divergence being at a small cairn a few yards short of the first stream after leaving the sheepfold.

The first mile is excellent, with first-class scenery all around. The route degenerates into dullness during the second mile although the final ridge of Blea Rigg is attractive and opens out new views.

ASCENT FROM DUNGEON GHYLL (via WHITEGILL CRAG)
1500 feet of ascent : 1½ miles from the New Hotel

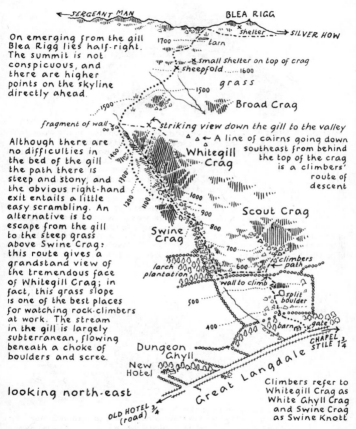

On emerging from the gill Blea Rigg lies half-right. The summit is not conspicuous, and there are higher points on the skyline directly ahead.

fragment of wall

Although there are no difficulties in the bed of the gill the path there is steep and stony, and the obvious right-hand exit entails a little easy scrambling. An alternative is to escape from the gill to the steep grass above Swine Crag: this route gives a grandstand view of the tremendous face of Whitegill Crag; in fact, this grass slope is one of the best places for watching rock-climbers at work. The stream in the gill is largely subterranean, flowing beneath a choke of boulders and scree.

looking north-east

striking view down the gill to the valley

A line of cairns going down southeast from behind the top of the crag is a climbers' route of descent

Climbers refer to Whitegill Crag as White Ghyll Crag and Swine Crag as Swine Knott

This is a walk for those who like to see grand rock-scenery at close quarters (from positions of absolute security!). On this route, Whitegill Crag reveals itself in almost shocking intimacy. The final stages are, in contrast, deadly dull.

THE SUMMIT

Although Blea Rigg is traversed on the popular ridge-walk from Silver How to Sergeant Man it gets little attention and the cairn, surmounting a rocky bluff, is often passed unnoticed. The rough top, however, with its many outcrops and small tarns, is entirely attractive, and the paths hereabouts (none of them very plain) are interesting to follow. The serrated top of Blea Crag, worthy of a cautious visit, is a hundred yards north of the summit cairn. Westwards, the ridge quickly rises to higher ground.

DESCENTS: The best route for Grasmere is via the ridge-path, rounding Lang How, and the obvious way down to Great Langdale is by the Stickle Tarn path, descending thence to Dungeon Ghyll. *In mist*, these paths are just about good enough to trace, thanks to many cairns, and should be followed closely. For Grasmere, in really bad weather, it is better to get off the ridge at once; take the quick route down to Easedale Tarn.

A: Main path, going down to Stickle Tarn.
B and C: Indistinct branches continuing ridge-walk to Sergeant Man.
   C gives a dramatic view of Blea Crag (✳); when it fades away turn up left to join B.
D: An ingenious track making use of a grassy rake immediately behind the edge of Blea Crag. (Quickest route, Stickle Tarn − Easedale Tarn)
E: Best way down to Easedale Tarn; path indistinct initially.
F: Path direct to old refreshment hut at Easedale Tarn; swampy.
G: Ridge-path to Grasmere or Silver How.   H: Junction indistinct.

THE VIEW

The view is good, although it contains none of the Scafell group nor the western fells. Prominent in an interesting panorama, due west, is the striking outline of Harrison Stickle and Pavey Ark: these heights are, however, better seen from several other points further along the ridge, westwards. Only a small part of Easedale Tarn is visible from the cairn; to obtain a birds-eye view of it, visit the top rocks of Blea Crag, north.

Principal Fells

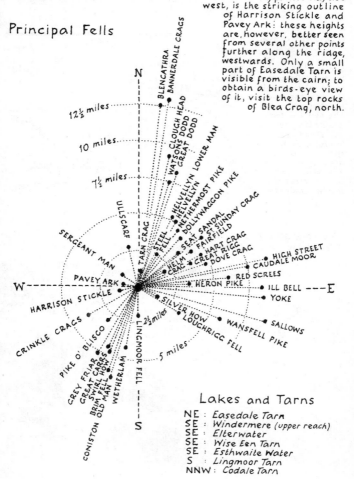

Lakes and Tarns

NE : *Easedale Tarn*
SE : *Windermere (upper reach)*
SE : *Elterwater*
SE : *Wise Een Tarn*
SE : *Esthwaite Water*
S : *Lingmoor Tarn*
NNW : *Codale Tarn*

RIDGE ROUTE

To SERGEANT MAN, 2414': WNW, then NW and W
1½ miles : *Minor depressions only : 700 feet of ascent*
A gradual climb along an interesting ridge

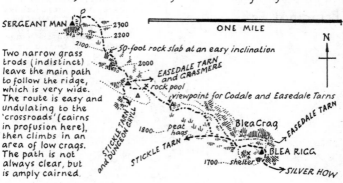

SERGEANT MAN ▲ ---- 2300
---- 2200
---- 2100

ONE MILE

N

50 foot rock slab at an easy inclination

2000

EASEDALE TARN
and GRASMERE

Two narrow grass
trods (indistinct)
leave the main path
to follow the ridge,
which is very wide.
The route is easy and
undulating to the
'crossroads' (cairns
in profusion here),
then climbs in an
area of low crags.
The path is not
always clear, but
is amply cairned.

rock pool

viewpoint for Codale and Easedale Tarns

STICKLE TARN and DUNGEON GHYLL

Blea Crag

EASEDALE TARN

1800 .... peat
hags

STICKLE TARN

BLEA RIGG

1700 .... shelter

SILVER HOW

*The rock-pool on the ridge
and the route beyond*

SERGEANT MAN

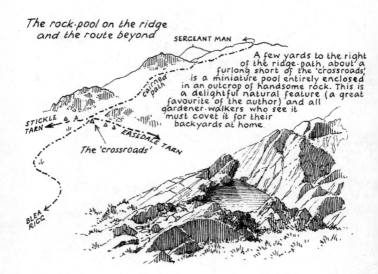

cairned path

A few yards to the right
of the ridge-path, about a
furlong short of the 'crossroads'
is a miniature pool entirely enclosed
in an outcrop of handsome rock. This is
a delightful natural feature (a great
favourite of the author) and all
gardener-walkers who see it
must covet it for their
backyards at home.

STICKLE
TARN

EASEDALE TARN

The 'crossroads'

BLEA
RIGG

RIDGE ROUTE

To SILVER HOW, 1292' : S, then ESE and E
2 miles : Several depressions : 150 feet of ascent
An easy, undulating walk, with many fine views.

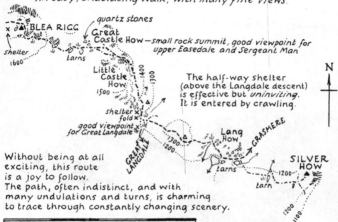

quartz stones

x ▲ BLEA RIGG

Great Castle How —*small rock summit, good viewpoint for upper Easedale and Sergeant Man*

shelter
1600

tarns

Little Castle How

1500

1400

1300

shelter
fold
good viewpoint for Great Langdale

GREAT LANGDALE

1300
1200

The half-way shelter (above the Langdale descent) is effective but *uninviting.*
It is entered by crawling.

N

Lang How

CRASMERE

SILVER HOW

1200

tarns

tarn

1200

1100

Without being at all exciting, this route is a joy to follow.
The path, often indistinct, and with many undulations and turns, is charming to trace through constantly changing scenery.

ONE MILE

The Shelter Stone on the top of Blea Rigg
This useful refuge is situated at the base of the prominent rocky tor 150 yards west of the summit-cairn. It cannot be seen from the path. The accommodation is strictly limited.

Calf Crag

1762'

Wythburn

ULLSCARF ▲

CALF
CRAG ▲

STEEL
FELL ▲

HIGH ▲
RAISE

HELM ▲
CRAG

Grasmere ●

MILES
0 1 2 3 4

*from the boulders
below Deer Bield Crag*

NATURAL FEATURES

The familiar pyramid of Helm Crag, rising sharply from the green fields of Grasmere, is the terminus of a ridge that curves away westwards to culminate finally in the rocky crest of a lesser-known eminence, Calf Crag. Beyond this point the characteristics of the ridge change, and sprawling slopes fall in easy gradients to the marshy flats of the Wyth Burn, the western boundary. The flanks of the fell, however, descend much more steeply and roughly in shelves of broken crag to the Greenburn valley, north, and Far Easedale, south. The county boundary traverses the broad top, coinciding with the limit of the Thirlmere catchment area, but the highest point is wholly within Westmorland.

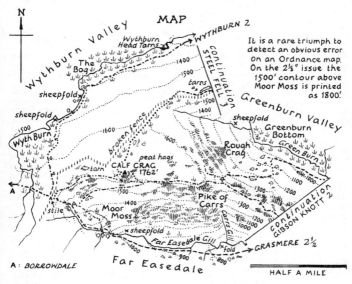

It is a rare triumph to detect an obvious error on an Ordnance map. On the 2½" issue the 1500' contour above Moor Moss is printed as 1800'.

A : BORROWDALE

HALF A MILE

Tourists bound for Borrowdale from Grasmere via Far Easedale should observe particularly that the Greenup crossing, between High Raise and Ullscarf, is to be found almost a mile *beyond* the stile at the head of Far Easedale and 350' higher, *in the same general direction, trending left*. The natural tendency is to turn down the valley on the right (Wythburn) under the impression that the pass has been crossed. This is a bad trap in misty weather on a first visit.

ASCENT FROM GRASMERE (via FAR EASEDALE)
1650 feet of ascent : 4½ miles

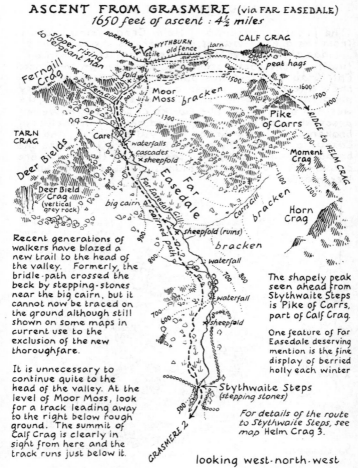

looking west·north·west

Recent generations of walkers have blazed a new trail to the head of the valley. Formerly, the bridle-path crossed the beck by stepping-stones near the big cairn, but it cannot now be traced on the ground although still shown on some maps in current use to the exclusion of the new thoroughfare.

It is unnecessary to continue quite to the head of the valley. At the level of Moor Moss, look for a track leading away to the right below rough ground. The summit of Calf Crag is clearly in sight from here and the track runs just below it.

The shapely peak seen ahead from Stythwaite Steps is Pike of Carrs, part of Calf Crag.

One feature of Far Easedale deserving mention is the fine display of berried holly each winter

For details of the route to Stythwaite Steps, see map Helm Crag 3.

Far Easedale is a beautiful and interesting valley with impressive rock scenery. The path along it is commonly used as a route to Borrowdale but can be conveniently adapted as a simple way onto Calf Crag. Far Easedale is wet underfoot in many places, always.

ASCENT FROM GRASMERE (via GREEN BURN)
1650 feet of ascent : 4½ miles

CALF CRAG

broken fence → STEEL FELL

1600
1500
1400
1300
1200
old path

slopes above Far Easedale

Pike of Carrs

Rough Crag

x sheepfold

STEEL FELL

vegetation-crowned big boulder

bracken

1000

RIDGE TO HELM CRAG

1300

1200

1100

GIBSON KNOTT

Indistinct (turn up before big boulder is reached)

bracken

moraines

Green Burn

moraines

Greenburn Bottom —

a surprising place, apparently the bed of a glacial lake, now a flat swamp amongst moraines

sheepfold (with massive corners) x

sheepfold (in ruins; enclosure of unusual (oval) shape)

The dead bracken makes a colourful scene here in winter.

During the initial part of the walk along the valley the summit rocks of Helm Crag (behind, up on the left) assume a strange variety of shapes in silhouette, changing outline with every few paces. Most prominent is the Lion and Lamb group, looking less familiar from this angle.

Greenburn Valley

900

dam

800

700

600

500

400

gate

STEEL FELL

two old cottages

gate

This route is less suitable for descent, — the top of the old path may not be easy to locate, and, in any case, the ridge offers a far more exhilarating return to Grasmere.

Gill Foot

GRASMERE (ROAD) 1¼

TOWN HEAD

looking west-north-west

Reach Gill Foot from Grasmere via Low Mill Bridge (see map Helm Crag 3)

This route is included mainly to introduce a valley that is unfrequented yet deserving of attention. It has also the advantage of the guidance of an old path almost to the ridge just below the summit.

ASCENT FROM WYTHBURN
1250 feet of ascent · 4 miles from Wythburn Church

CALF CRAG
1700

FAR EASEDALE
(for GRASMERE)

slopes rising to High Raise

GREENUP EDGE
(for BORROWDALE)

stile
gateway

1600

Here, as elsewhere, light-coloured grass (almost white) indicates firm ground. Keep away from red grass, rushes and patches of green mosses.

peat hags

1500

sheepfold

waterfall
boulders
sheepfold

The Bog

broken fence

STEEL FELL

'The Bog' (with a capital T & B deservedly) is the official name of this morass. It may be said that here, at any rate, the foot of man has never trod (if it has, it must have made a horribly squelching sound!). The beck flows sluggishly and silently in a swamp.

The first moraine above the waterfalls stands like a sentinel at the entrance to the strange upper valley

moraines

Wythburn Head Tarns (an ambitious name for slight widenings of the beck into pools)

a particularly big boulder

1300

waterfall
waterfall
waterfall

Rake Crags

Black Crag

bracken

1000
1100
900

sheepfold

800

gate

700

gate

Scenically, this is the best half-mile in the valley, with the beck tumbling in a rocky bed to a wooded ravine.

The imposing rocky rampart overlooking the valley on the north-west is Nab Crags, a shoulder of Ullscarf.

Wyth Burn

looking south-west

gates

Steel End

Primarily this route is included to serve as an introduction to the Wythburn valley: the climbing of Calf Crag is incidental and is suggested only to provide an objective. The valley, besides being a supreme study in desolation (especially in rain and mist) has many geological and geographical features of unusual interest.

One visit will be enough for most folk, however, for the ground is abominably and unescapably WET

GRASMERE 3¾

MAIN ROAD

signpost (spells Wythburn 'Wÿthburn')

ROAD TO ARMBOTH

Thirlmere

WYTHBURN CHURCH ½

THE SUMMIT

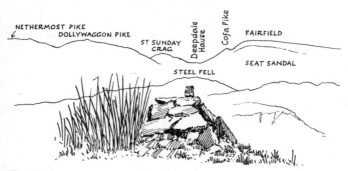

The highest point, small and rocky, is a pleasant place for a halt and quiet contemplation of the scenery. Sheep think so, too, and wearers of new clothes should not sink into repose here without first clearing away the profuse evidences of their occupation. A feature unusual on summits is a clump of rushes, abutting on the neat cairn. Immediately below the cairn, on the south, is a wall of crag that constitutes a danger in mist.

DESCENTS: The best route of descent, full of interest, keeps to the ridge over Helm Crag and so down to Grasmere. The path going off the top into the Greenburn valley is not easy to find. *In mist and bad weather*, it is advisable to retire to the shelter afforded by Far Easedale, reached by walking north of west (the rushes side of the cairn) for 200 yards and following the fence to the step-stile at the head of the valley, where turn down left.

The summit crags
(the maximum height is about 35 feet)

THE VIEW

The best feature in a moderate and restricted view is a beautiful vista of the Vale of Grasmere with Far Easedale curving into it from the inexpressibly wild flanks of Tarn Crag and Sergeant Man nearby: a complete contrast in landscapes in the space of two miles.

Principal Fells

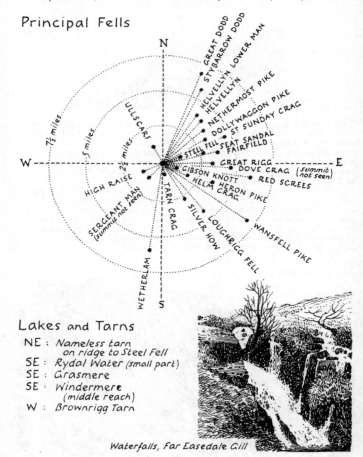

N

GREAT DODD
STYBARROW DODD
HELVELLYN LOWER MAN
HELVELLYN
NETHERMOST PIKE
DOLLYWAGGON PIKE
ST SUNDAY CRAG
SEAT SANDAL
FAIRFIELD
STEEL FELL
GREAT RIGG
DOVE CRAG *(summit not seen)*
GIBSON KNOTT
RED SCREES
HELM CRAG
HERON PIKE
SILVER HOW
LOUGHRIGG FELL
WANSFELL PIKE

ULLSCARF

W ———————— E

HIGH RAISE

SERGEANT MAN *(summit not seen)*

TARN CRAG

WETHERLAM

S

7½ miles
5 miles
2½ miles

Lakes and Tarns

NE : *Nameless tarn on ridge to Steel Fell*
SE : *Rydal Water (small part)*
SE : *Grasmere*
SE : *Windermere (middle reach)*
W : *Brownrigg Tarn*

Waterfalls, Far Easedale Gill

RIDGE ROUTES

To STEEL FELL, 1811' : 1½ miles : NE, curving E to ESE
Main depression at 1535' : 350 feet of ascent
An easy walk, with fence as guide, but very marshy initially

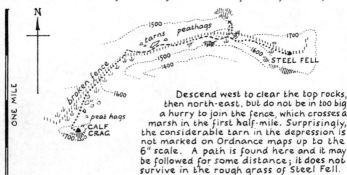

Descend west to clear the top rocks, then north-east, but do not be in too big a hurry to join the fence, which crosses a marsh in the first half-mile. Surprisingly, the considerable tarn in the depression is not marked on Ordnance maps up to the 6" scale. A path is found here and it may be followed for some distance; it does not survive in the rough grass of Steel Fell.

To GIBSON KNOTT, 1379' : 1¼ miles : E, then ESE
Several minor depressions : 100 feet of ascent
An interesting path, a beautiful walk, and splendid views

Pike of Carrs

From the summit a path can be seen running below the crags on the Easedale side : it may be joined by a wide detour and followed without difficulty, although intermittent, to Gibson Knott. The path keeps below the ridge; the crest may be followed instead but is a long succession of trivial ups and downs. If the path is adhered to too closely, however, the cairn on Gibson Knott will be missed — it stands on a rocky mound 30 yards to the left.

Eagle Crag

- Rosthwaite
- Stonethwaite

▲ ▲ ULLSCARF
EAGLE CRAG

▲ HIGH RAISE

MILES
0   1   2   3

from Stonethwaite Beck

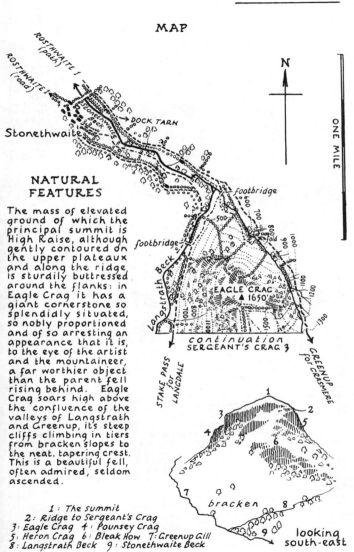

MAP

ROSTHWAITE 1 (path)

ROSTHWAITE 1 (road)

Stonethwaite

DOCK TARN

footbridge

footbridge

600

500

700

800

900

1000

1100

1200

1300

fold

EAGLE CRAG ▲ 1650'

Langstrath Beck

N

ONE MILE

continuation
SERGEANT'S CRAG 3

STAKE PASS *for* LANGDALE

GREENUP *for* GRASMERE

NATURAL FEATURES

The mass of elevated ground of which the principal summit is High Raise, although gently contoured on the upper plateaux and along the ridge is sturdily buttressed around the flanks: in Eagle Crag it has a giant cornerstone so splendidly situated, so nobly proportioned and of so arresting an appearance that it is, to the eye of the artist and the mountaineer, a far worthier object than the parent fell rising behind. Eagle Crag soars high above the confluence of the valleys of Langstrath and Greenup, its steep cliffs climbing in tiers from bracken slopes to the neat, tapering crest. This is a beautiful fell, often admired, seldom ascended.

bracken

looking south-east

1 : The summit
2 : Ridge to Sergeant's Crag
3 : Eagle Crag   4 : Pounsey Crag
5 : Heron Crag   6 : Bleak How   7 : Greenup Gill
8 : Langstrath Beck   9 : Stonethwaite Beck

ASCENT FROM STONETHWAITE
1300 feet of ascent : 2 miles

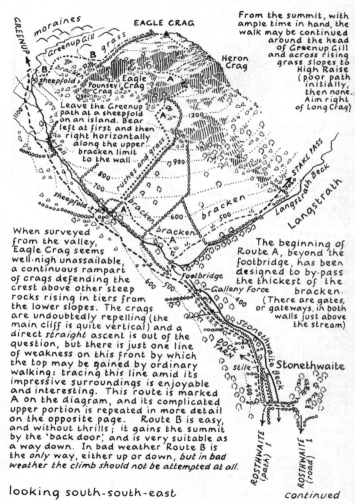

From the summit, with ample time in hand, the walk may be continued around the head of Greenup Gill and across rising grass slopes to High Raise (poor path initially, then none. Aim right of Long Crag)

Leave the Greenup path at a sheepfold on an island. Bear left at first and then right horizontally along the upper bracken limit to the wall.

The beginning of Route A, beyond the footbridge, has been designed to by-pass the thickest of the bracken. (There are gates, or gateways, in both walls just above the stream)

When surveyed from the valley, Eagle Crag seems well-nigh unassailable, a continuous rampart of crags defending the crest above other steep rocks rising in tiers from the lower slopes. The crags are undoubtedly repelling (the main cliff is quite vertical) and a direct *straight* ascent is out of the question, but there is just one line of weakness on this front by which the top may be gained by ordinary walking: tracing this line amid its impressive surroundings is enjoyable and interesting. This route is marked A on the diagram, and its complicated upper portion is repeated in more detail on the opposite page. Route B is easy, and without thrills; it gains the summit by the 'back door', and is very suitable as a way down. In bad weather Route B is the *only* way, either up or down, *but in bad weather the climb should not be attempted at all.*

looking south-south-east

continued

ASCENT FROM STONETHWAITE

continued

The upper section of Route A

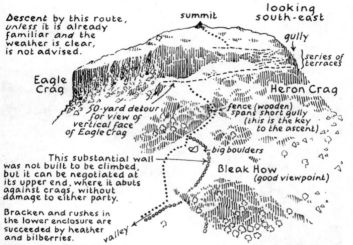

looking south-east

Descent by this route, *unless* it is already familiar *and* the weather is clear, is not advised.

summit

gully

series of terraces

Eagle Crag

Heron Crag

50-yard detour for view of vertical face of Eagle Crag

fence (wooden) spans short gully (this is the key to the ascent)

big boulders

This substantial wall was not built to be climbed, but it can be negotiated at its upper end, where it abuts against crags, without damage to either party.

Bleak How (good viewpoint)

Bracken and rushes in the lower enclosure are succeeded by heather and bilberries.

valley

Here, and in other craggy places, sheep should be disturbed as little as possible, even at inconvenience to the walker; otherwise they may become casualties. The walls are not put there for ornament: they serve a vital purpose, and if stones are displaced they should be put back, and firmly.

Eagle Crag is the most distinctive object in the Stonethwaite landscape and its ascent reveals all the beauty of the valley in a pleasant half-day's (or summer evening's) expedition.

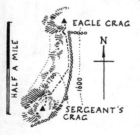

EAGLE CRAG

HALF A MILE

N

1600

SERGEANT'S CRAG

RIDGE ROUTE

To SERGEANT'S CRAG, 1873'
½ mile : S. then SSW
Minor depressions
250 feet of ascent
Easy, but not safe in mist

A rough little path leads down to the head of a gully at the wall-corner. Do not cross the wall, but accompany it south, finally inclining away from it.

THE SUMMIT

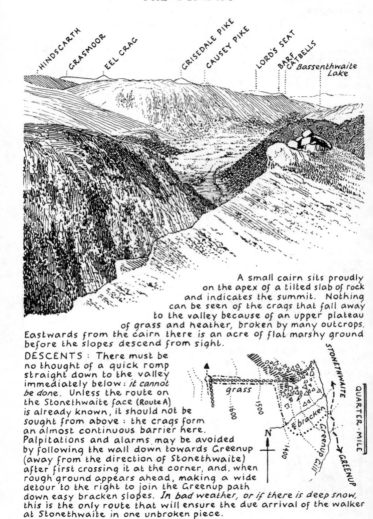

HINDSCARTH GRASMOOR EEL CRAG GRISEDALE PIKE CAUSEY PIKE LORD'S SEAT BARF CATBELLS Bassenthwaite Lake

A small cairn sits proudly
on the apex of a tilted slab of rock
and indicates the summit. Nothing
can be seen of the crags that fall away
to the valley because of an upper plateau
of grass and heather, broken by many outcrops.
Eastwards from the cairn there is an acre of flat marshy ground
before the slopes descend from sight.

DESCENTS : There must be
no thought of a quick romp
straight down to the valley
immediately below: *it cannot
be done*. Unless the route on
the Stonethwaite face (Route A)
is already known, it should not be
sought from above : the crags form
an almost continuous barrier here.
Palpitations and alarms may be avoided
by following the wall down towards Greenup
(away from the direction of Stonethwaite)
after first crossing it at the corner, and, when
rough ground appears ahead, making a wide
detour to the right to join the Greenup path
down easy bracken slopes. *In bad weather, or if there is deep snow,
this is the only route that will ensure the due arrival of the walker
at Stonethwaite in one unbroken piece.*

THE VIEW

Principal Fells

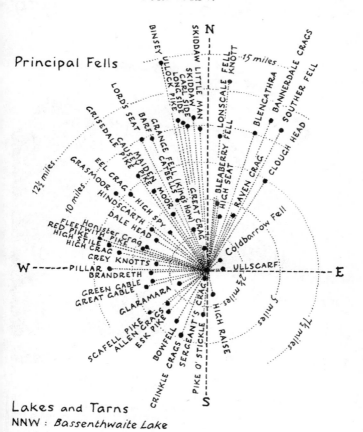

Lakes and Tarns
NNW : *Bassenthwaite Lake*

The view of the Stonethwaite valley, which might be expected
to be excellent, is not quite that, the summit being set rather
too far back from the edge of the crags to enable all of it to
be seen; a short and easy descent of the upper slope leads to
better points of vantage. But generally the valley is too short
to be really effective in a view, although the whole picture is
very pleasing to west and north. Eastwards the scene is drab.

Gibson Knott 1379'

from Helm Crag

STEEL FELL ▲

CALF CRAG ▲   ▲ GIBSON KNOTT

HELM CRAG ▲

Grasmere •

MILES
0   1   2   3

Gibson Knott is the most elevated of the several sundry knobs and bumps that form the crest of the mile-long ridge linking at its extremities Calf Crag and Helm Crag and dividing the valleys of Far Easedale and Greenburn. There is much rock in evidence along the serrated top and fringing steep flanks; in particular, a prominent buttress, Horn Crag, adorned with juniper, rises from the bracken of the Easedale slope. The summit is interesting, other parts less so. The fellsides are 'dry', draining without forming regular watercourses.

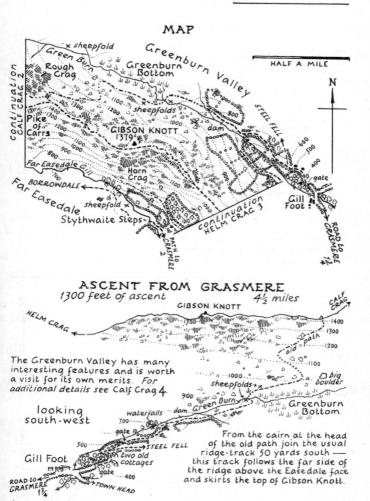

MAP

Greenburn Valley

× sheepfold
Green Burn
Rough Crag
Greenburn Bottom

HALF A MILE

N

continuation CALF CRAG 2

Pike of Carrs

GIBSON KNOTT 1319

sheepfolds

dam

STEEL FELL

gate

Far Easedale Gill

Horn Crag

BORROWDALE

Far Easedale

sheepfold ×
Stythwaite Steps

continuation HELM CRAG 3

Gill Foot

ROAD TO GRASMERE 1½

PATH TO GRASMERE 2

ASCENT FROM GRASMERE
1300 feet of ascent   4½ miles

CALF CRAG

GIBSON KNOTT

1400
1300
old path
1200
1100

HELM CRAG

1000

The Greenburn Valley has many interesting features and is worth a visit for its own merits. For additional details see Calf Crag 4.

sheepfolds ×

big boulder

900 Green Burn

dam

Greenburn Bottom

looking south-west

waterfalls

gate STEEL FELL

500

two old cottages

Gill Foot

gate

ROAD TO GRASMERE 1¾

TOWN HEAD

400

From the cairn at the head of the old path join the usual ridge-track 50 yards south — this track follows the far side of the ridge above the Easedale face and skirts the top of Gibson Knott.

Although the usual (and best) route lies along the ridge from Helm Crag, it is suggested that this be reserved for descent and the route illustrated be used as a way up: it is full of interest and has the advantage of a path so easily graduated that the ascent is better described as a walk than a climb.

THE SUMMIT

It was categorically stated, two pages ago, that Gibson Knott is the highest point on the ridge. The observer on the spot will probably question this, for the next rise eastwards seems to be higher. Large-scale maps do not settle the doubt, and it is perhaps safer to say that Gibson Knott is the Ordnance Survey's only trigonometrical station on the ridge and that *usually* the most elevated point is selected. The summit is an abrupt rise, surmounted by a cairn above a smooth rock wall.

DESCENTS : Keep to the path along the ridge.   Descents direct from the summit into Far Easedale or Greenburn may lead to trouble.

RIDGE ROUTES

To CALF CRAG, 1762' : 1¼ miles : WNW, then W.
Several minor depressions : 450 feet of ascent
An interesting walk with good views of Far Easedale

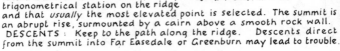

Join the path 30 yards south of the cairn and follow it west. With a few interruptions it continues to the base of the summit crags of Calf Crag, skirting the head of the prominent Pike of Carrs : interesting throughout, it keeps on the Easedale side of the ridge and is preferable to the actual crest, which is rather tedious.

To HELM CRAG, 1299'
1 mile : E, then SE
Depression at 1050'
320 feet of ascent
A delightful path

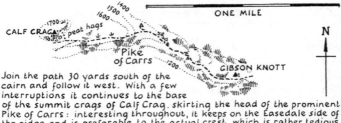

Join the path 30 yards south of the cairn and follow it east to the top of the next rise where it winds in and out and up and down in a charming manner before descending to the depression below Helm Crag, the curious top of which is reached by a stiff little climb.

ONE MILE

THE VIEW

The cairn is not quite the best viewpoint: the ridge eastwards is more satisfying. There is strong contrast between the smooth slopes towering across the Keswick road and the rough territory and serrated skyline across Far Easedale.

Principal Fells

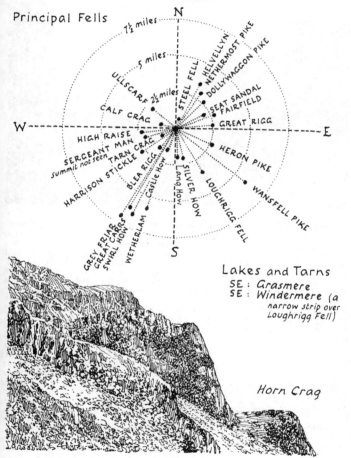

N

7½ miles
5 miles
2½ miles

ULLSCARF
STEEL FELL
HELVELLYN
NETHERMOST PIKE
DOLLYWAGGON PIKE
CALF CRAG
SEAT SANDAL
FAIRFIELD
W — — — — — — — — — — — — E
GREAT RIGG
HIGH RAISE
SERGEANT MAN
summit not seen
TARN CRAG
HERON PIKE
HARRISON STICKLE
BLEA RIGG
Castle How
SILVER HOW
Lang How
LOUGHRIGG FELL
WANSFELL PIKE
GREY FRIAR
GREAT CARRS
SWIRL HOW
WETHERLAM
S

Lakes and Tarns

SE: *Grasmere*
SE: *Windermere* (a narrow strip over Loughrigg Fell)

Horn Crag

Grange Fell

King's How, from Shepherds Crag

Grange Fell is nothing on the map, everything when beneath one's feet. In small compass, here is concentrated the beauty, romance, interest and excitement of the typical Lakeland scene. Here Nature has given of her very best and produced a loveliness that is exquisite. Not strictly the territory of fellwalkers, perhaps; yet those who consistently hurry past Grange Fell to get to grips with the Scafells and Gable would do well to turn aside to it once in a while, alone, and quietly walk its sylvan glades and heathery top. The exercise will not tire the limbs, but it will do the heart and spirit and faith of the walker a power of good, and gladden his eye exceedingly.

Rising abruptly between Borrowdale and Watendlath Beck, and split by that delightful little valley of trees, Troutdale, the fell is almost encircled by a grey girdle of crags half-hidden in rich foliage: below is the wreckage of centuries in the form of masses of boulders (one of which, the Bowder Stone, is famous) overgrown by lush bracken and screened by a forest of birches. The top of the fell is an up-and-down tangled plateau, from which rise three main summits: (1) Brund Fell, the highest; (2) King's How, deservedly the best-known; and (3) Ether Knot, behind a barricade of long heather.

Lodore

HIGH SEAT ▲

Grange ●

● GRANGE FELL ▲

● Watendlath

Rosthwaite ●

MILES

0   1   2   3

MAP

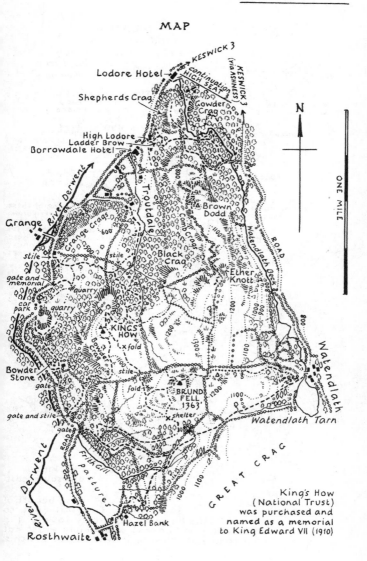

KESWICK 3

Lodore Hotel

continuation HIGH SEAT

Shepherds Crag

KESWICK 3 (via ASHNESS)

Gowder Crag

N

High Lodore
Ladder Brow
Borrowdale Hotel

ONE MILE

River Derwent

Troutdale

Brown Dodd

Grange

Grange Crag

600

Black Crag

Comb Gill

Watendlath Beck

stile

stile

ROAD

gate and memorial

Ether Knott

car park

quarry

quarry

1000

1000

800

KINGS HOW

x fold

1200

Watendlath

Bowder Stone

gate

stile

fold

BRUND FELL
1363

shelter

1200

1100

gate and stile

gate

x

Watendlath Tarn

River Derwent

ROAD

Frith Gill
pastures

1000

1100

GREAT CRAG

Rosthwaite

Hazel Bank

King's How
(National Trust)
was purchased and
named as a memorial
to King Edward VII (1910)

ASCENT FROM GRANGE

1300 feet of ascent
(1050, to King's How only)
2 miles; 2½ via Troutdale
(1¼ and 2 to King's How only)

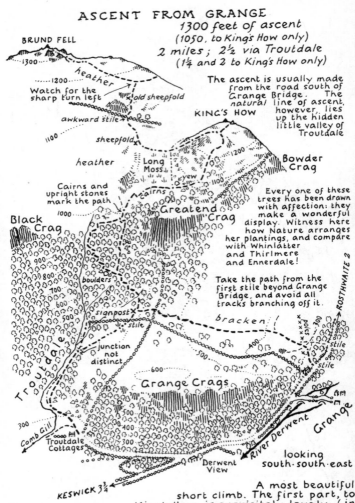

BRUND FELL
1300
heather
1200
Watch for the
sharp turn left
old sheepfold
awkward stile
1100
sheepfold
heather
Long
Moss
yew
1000
Cairns and
upright stones
mark the path
Black
Crag
900
800
700
600
boulders
signpost
stile
junction
not
distinct
Troutdale
300
Comb Gill
Troutdale
Cottages
500
400
300
600
500
400
300
KING'S HOW
1200
Greatend
Crag
cairns
Bowder
Crag
1100
bracken
400
500
600
Grange Crags
Derwent
View
ROSTHWAITE 2
300
stile
stile
River Derwent
Grange
looking
south·south·east
KESWICK 3¾

The ascent is usually made
from the road south of
Grange Bridge.   The
natural line of ascent,
however, lies
up the hidden
little valley of
Troutdale

Every one of these
trees has been drawn
with affection: they
make a wonderful
display.   Witness here
how Nature arranges
her plantings, and compare
with Whinlatter and Thirlmere
and Ennerdale!

Take the path from the
first stile beyond Grange
Bridge, and avoid all
tracks branching off it.

A most beautiful
short climb. The first part, to
King's How, is exquisitely lovely (in
autumn, a golden ladder to heaven) and simply must not
be missed. Sacrifice any other walk, if need be, but not this!

ASCENT FROM ROSTHWAITE
1100 feet of ascent to Brund Fell : 1½ or 2 miles
(1000 feet, 1½ miles, to King's How direct)

BRUND FELL

KING'S HOW

Bowder Crag

1300
heather
1200

1200
cairns
sheepfold
stile (awkward)
1100
Follow closely the line of cairns (especially in descent)
1000
900
1000
1100

gap
800
700
900
900
hut × (shelter)
800

bracken
400
bracken

WATENDLATH

KESWICK
bridle path
gate and stile together
gate and signpost (TO WATENDLATH)

600
gate
signpost (TO KESWICK ROAD)

Frith Wood
Yew Crag

Note here the water-depth indicators on the side of the road, which is liable to flooding

Frith Gill

River Derwent

Stonethwaite Beck

ROAD

Hazel Bank

Instead of using the familiar Watendlath path, try the quieter way in Frith Wood, or better still the bridle path above it, which is in some danger of neglect, undeservedly

Rosthwaite

looking north

The diagram gives separate routes for Brund Fell and King's How: if both summits are visited, as they should be, the alternative may be used for descent; the easier way round is to climb Brund Fell first.

This is an excellent little expedition, with splendid views, but is not suitable for a day of bad weather.

ASCENT FROM WATENDLATH
550 feet of ascent : 1 mile (to Brund Fell only)

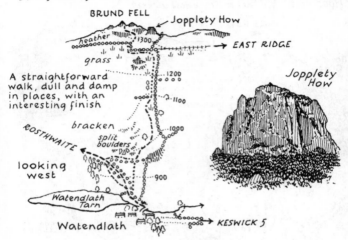

BRUND FELL → Jopplety How

→ EAST RIDGE

heather · 1300

grass

Jopplety How

A straightforward walk, dull and damp in places, with an interesting finish

1200

1100

ROSTHWAITE ←

bracken

split boulders · DOD

1000

looking west

900

Watendlath Tarn

Watendlath

→ KESWICK 5

THE EAST RIDGE

The east ridge of Grange Fell is not often visited, but gives an interesting and beautiful traverse, better done from south to north. The ridge starts to take shape at Jopplety How and a fence may be followed over marshy ground (no path) to Ether Knott, the most prominent peak on the ridge, which here alters its character and becomes rough and heathery, a wall taking over the duties of the fence; the easiest walking is alongside it. Beyond, on Brown Dodd, the wall ends abruptly on the edge of crags, where a path takes shape and makes a sporting crossing of very steep ground. Escape from the escarpments hereabouts is effected down a rough gully (cairns) and, a little further, the tourist path descending Ladder Brow to High Lodore is met, but having come so far the walker should certainly complete the ridge by visiting the top of Shepherds Crag, a lovely belvedere occasionally profaned by the rich language of climbers on the cliff directly below.

Both sides of the east ridge have steep crags, continuous in the middle section. Overlooking the valley of Watendlath Beck is the gloomy wall of Caffell Side, while Comb Crags extend in an unbroken line above the trees of Troutdale.

The ridge is easily accessible from Brund Fell, but to force a way to it direct from King's How involves a laborious struggle in a tangle of thick heather. It offers a good return route to Grange or Lodore from Brund Fell (in clear weather) — but not for pedestrians who prefer simple walking on distinct paths.

THE SUMMIT

The summit of BRUND FELL is one of exceptional interest. A number of steep-sided rock towers rise oddly from the heathery top; enthusiastic rock-scramblers will enjoy sampling them all, while less active walkers will find much fascinating detail in a perambulation of this unusual summit. A cairn identifies the highest tower.

SKIDDAW

Derwentwater →

The summit of KING'S HOW, in contrast, is a steep-sided dome, rising abruptly to a bare top with two cairns.

DESCENTS: King's How is so encircled by craggy ground that descent by the paths is imperative even in the best of weather. The lesser and lower of the two cairns marks the start of the path to Grange; the Rosthwaite path leaves in the opposite direction (south) where a line of cairns is found. Brund Fell, too, is better descended by its paths, intermittent though they are, but in bad weather a safe and quick way to the Rosthwaite–Watendlath path may be made alongside the wall running south from Jopplety How, first crossing it.

THE SUMMIT WALK
BETWEEN
KING'S HOW and BRUND FELL

GRANGE

·1200·

KING'S HOW

ROSTHWAITE

1100

* sheepfold

awkward stile

old sheepfold

Watch for this junction (easily missed)

ROSTHWAITE

1000

BRUND FELL
·1300·

EAST RIDGE

Jopplety How

WATENDLATH

HALF A MILE

N

Leave King's How by the Grange path, but, almost at once, where the path swings left, turn *right* to descend a grassy rake.

THE VIEW

Principal Fells

The views from the two main summits are very much alike, that from Brund Fell being a little more extensive but not so beautiful as that from King's How, the latter benefiting by a closer proximity to Borrowdale.

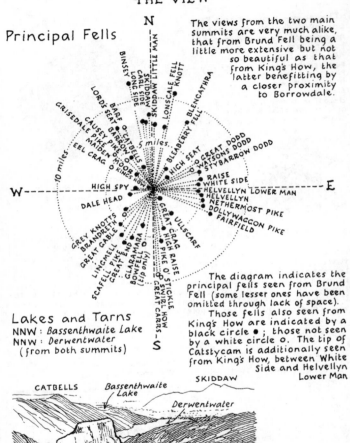

N

NNW
LITTLE MAN
SKIDDAW
BINSEY
LONG SIDE
SKIDDAW
LOW DOOR
LONSCALE FELL
KNOTT
BLENCATHRA
BARF o.CATBELLS
LORDS SEAT
CAUSEY PIKE o.
GRISEDALE PIKE o.
MAIDEN MOOR
EEL CRAG
o.KINGS HOW
BLEABERRY FELL
HIGH SEAT
o. GREAT DODD
o. WATSONS DODD
STYBARROW DODD
RAISE
WHITE SIDE
HELVELLYN LOWER MAN
HELVELLYN
NETHERMOST PIKE
DOLLYWAGGON PIKE
FAIRFIELD
HIGH SPY
DALE HEAD
GREY KNOTTS
BRANDRETH o.
GREAT GABLE
LINGMELL
GREAT END
GLARAMARA o.
SCAFELL PIKE
GREAT PIKE
BOWFELL o.
o.ROSTHWAITE
GREAT CARRS
GREAT CRAG
HIGH RAISE
PIKE O'STICKLE
SWIRL HOW
ULLSCARF

5 miles

10 miles

W

E

S

The diagram indicates the principal fells seen from Brund Fell (some lesser ones have been omitted through lack of space).

Those fells also seen from King's How are indicated by a black circle ● ; those not seen by a white circle o. The tip of Catstycam is additionally seen from King's How, between White Side and Helvellyn Lower Man

Lakes and Tarns
NNW: Bassenthwaite Lake
NNW: Derwentwater
(from both summits)

CATBELLS
Bassenthwaite Lake
SKIDDAW
Derwentwater

looking north from the top of Brund Fell

The north ridge of King's How with Skiddaw in the background

Borrowdale, from the lower slopes of Brund Fell

Great Crag

from Watendlath

Between the deep Stonethwaite valley and the shallow depression containing Bleatarn Gill rises an indefinite and complex mass of rough undulating ground, a place of craggy and wooded slopes, of heathery tors and mossy swamps and shy little tarns — a beautiful labyrinth, a joy to the explorer but the despair of the map-maker. Nestling here is Dock Tarn, a jewel deserving a sweeter name, in a surround of rocky heights of which Great Crag is the most pronounced, and the natural summit of the fell — although perhaps not quite the highest point. Its altitude is not given on Ordnance maps, nor a 1500' contour, but the cairn can be little below this height, if at all.

Great Crag is one of those modest fells which seldom seem to invite attention, and few people know it by name, yet many are they who have trodden its lower slopes on the popular path of the pilgrims journeying to Watendlath from Rosthwaite.

Lakeland is not usually associated with heather — but here it thrives with a tropical vigour, and walking in it is arduous and difficult.

• Watendlath
• Rosthwaite
▲ GREAT CRAG
• Stonethwaite

▲ ULLSCARF

MILES
0   1   2   3   4

MAP

Footbridge, Bleatarn Gill

ASCENT FROM STONETHWAITE
1200 feet of ascent : 1½ miles

GREAT CRAG

path goes on to WATENDLATH

heather

Dock Tarn

heather

tarn

1400

× ruin

1200

sheepfold

tarn

1300

1300

Knotts

High Crag

1200

White Crag

1100

1000

Willygrass Gill

× butt × ruin

Watch for squirrels in the wood

800

falls 700

signpost

WYTHBURN (according to the signpost, but see note Ullscarf 8)

stile

500

Great Crag never appears in view conspicuously on this route, and locating the highest point (which has a good cairn) amongst the several sundry undulations is an interesting problem. There is no continuous path to the cairn, but it is fun to link up the many intermittent tracks in the heather, and worth doing because, away from the tracks, the ground is rough and walking difficult. The only *good* path on the fell is the one skirting Dock Tarn.

ROSTHWAITE (path) 1

signpost (unstable; don't depend on it)

stile

GREENUP

400

Stonethwaite Beck

ROSTHWAITE (road) 1

Stonethwaite

signpost

looking north-east

This is a most beautiful short climb, best done on a sunny day in August, for then the upper slopes are ablaze with heather, Dock Tarn is a place to lie adreaming, and life seems a sweet sweet thing.

Dock Tarn

ASCENT FROM WATENDLATH
700 feet of ascent : 1½ miles

If the sun is in the sky and the heather in bloom, on no account fail to make the short detour to Dock Tarn after visiting the top.

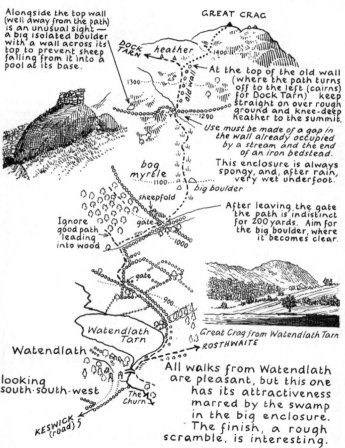

GREAT CRAG

Alongside the top wall (well away from the path) is an unusual sight — a big isolated boulder with a wall across its top to prevent sheep falling from it into a pool at its base.

DOCK TARN heather

1400

1300

old wall

1200

At the top of the old wall (where the path turns off to the left (cairns) for Dock Tarn) keep straight on over rough ground and knee-deep heather to the summit.

Use must be made of a gap in the wall already occupied by a stream and the end of an iron bedstead.

This enclosure is always spongy, and, after rain, very wet underfoot.

bog myrtle

1100

big boulder

sheepfold

gate

1000

Ignore good path leading into wood

After leaving the gate the path is indistinct for 200 yards. Aim for the big boulder, where it becomes clear.

gate

900

Watendlath Tarn

Great Crag from Watendlath Tarn

Watendlath

ROSTHWAITE

looking south-south-west

The Churn

KESWICK (road)

All walks from Watendlath are pleasant, but this one has its attractiveness marred by the swamp in the big enclosure. The finish, a rough scramble, is interesting.

THE SUMMIT

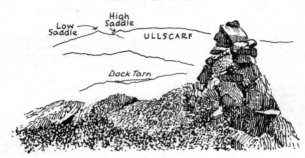

Low Saddle · High Saddle · ULLSCARF

Dock Tarn

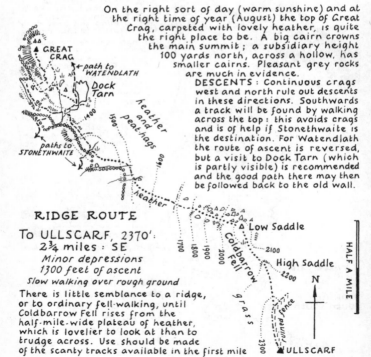

On the right sort of day (warm sunshine) and at the right time of year (August) the top of Great Crag, carpeted with lovely heather, is quite the right place to be. A big cairn crowns the main summit; a subsidiary height 100 yards north, across a hollow, has smaller cairns. Pleasant grey rocks are much in evidence.

DESCENTS: Continuous crags west and north rule out descents in these directions. Southwards a track will be found by walking across the top: this avoids crags and is of help if Stonethwaite is the destination. For Watendlath the route of ascent is reversed, but a visit to Dock Tarn (which is partly visible) is recommended and the good path there may then be followed back to the old wall.

GREAT CRAG
path to WATENDLATH
Dock Tarn
1400
1500
paths to STONETHWAITE
heather and peat-hags
1600
heather
Low Saddle
Coldbarrow Fell
High Saddle
1700
1800
1900
2000
2100
2200
Coldbarrow grass
ruined fence
2300
ULLSCARF
N
HALF A MILE

RIDGE ROUTE

To ULLSCARF, 2370':
2¾ miles : SE
Minor depressions
1300 feet of ascent
Slow walking over rough ground

There is little semblance to a ridge, or to ordinary fell-walking, until Coldbarrow Fell rises from the half-mile-wide plateau of heather, which is lovelier to look at than to trudge across. Use should be made of the scanty tracks available in the first mile

THE VIEW

The view is pleasing, without being extensive, the best of many interesting features being the green strath of upper Borrowdale backed by the towering heights of Great Gable and the Scafells. A better picture of Watendlath is obtained from the lower summit to the north.

Principal Fells

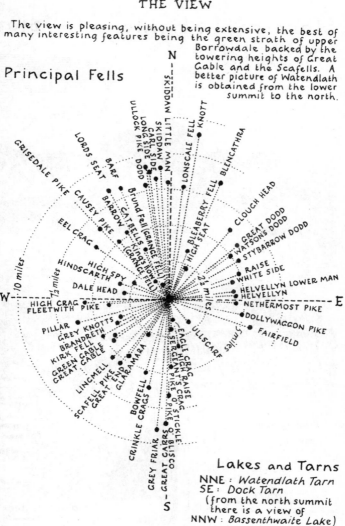

Lakes and Tarns

NNE: *Watendlath Tarn*
SE: *Dock Tarn*
(from the north summit there is a view of
NNW: *Bassenthwaite Lake*)

Harrison Stickle 2403'

the highest of the Langdale Pikes

HIGH RAISE ▲

PIKE O'
STICKLE ▲ ▲ HARRISON
STICKLE
LOFT CRAG ● New
Old Hotel ● ● Hotel
Dungeon Ghyll

MILES

0   1   2   3

from Great Langdale Beck

NATURAL FEATURES

No mountain profile in Lakeland arrests and excites the attention more than that of the Langdale Pikes and no mountain group better illustrates the dramatic appeal of a sudden rising of the vertical from the horizontal; the full height from valley to summit is revealed at a glance in one simple abrupt upsurge to all travellers on the distant shore of Windermere and, more intimately, on the beautiful approach along Great Langdale. Nor is the appeal visual only: that steep ladder to heaven stirs the imagination, and even the emotions, and this is especially so whenever the towering peaks come into view suddenly and unexpectedly.   The difference in altitude between top and base is little more than 2000 feet, yet, because it occurs in a distance laterally of only three-quarters of a mile, it is enough to convey a remarkable impression of remoteness, of inaccessibility, to the craggy summits surmounting the rugged slopes.

continued

NATURAL FEATURES

continued

Of the group of peaks known collectively as Langdale Pikes, the highest is Harrison Stickle, and this is the fell that presents such a bold front to, and dominates, the middle curve of the valley. It is severed from its satellites westwards by the deep gloomy ravines of Dungeon Ghyll, which, at a lower altitude and near its famous waterfall, turns across the bottom slopes towards Mill Gill, the eastern boundary, so that the fell's actual footing in the valley is quite small, only the width of a field. The ridged summit is liberally buttressed by crags, as is a curious shoulder running down to the hanging valley occupied by Stickle Tarn, a considerable sheet of water no less attractive for being partly artificial.

The uninitiated climber who scales Harrison Stickle from Langdale expecting to find the northerly slopes descending as steeply as those he has just ascended will be surprised to see, on reaching the main cairn, that higher ground continues beyond a very shallow depression. The Pikes are, in fact, no more than the abrupt termination of a wide ridge coming down from High Raise, and on this side their aspect, in contrast, is one of almost comical insignificance. But let nothing derogatory be said of Harrison Stickle. The majesty and masculine strength of the Langdale front is itself quite enough to establish the fell as a firm favourite with all, even with those admirers who are content to stand on the road below and gape upwards, while for those who set forth to conquer, it provides a very worthy climb indeed.

looking
north-west

1 : The summit
2 : Ridge continuing to
    Thunacar Knott and High Raise
3 : Pike How   4 : Miller Crag
5 : Stickle Tarn   6 : Mill Gill
7 : Dungeon Ghyll
8 : Dungeon Ghyll Force
9 : Great Langdale Beck

The Ravines of Dungeon Ghyll

The upper ravine
between Thorn Crag
and Harrison Stickle

The middle ravine. The waterfall (on the right), which terminates this section, falls into a rock basin and escapes over a breach in the lip to form a second fall — a most charming scene, revealed only by a close visit (which entails some scrambling).

The lower ravine

Hidden amongst the trees is Dungeon Ghyll Force, a much-frequented waterfall (that does not compare, as an object of beauty, with the little-frequented one mentioned above).

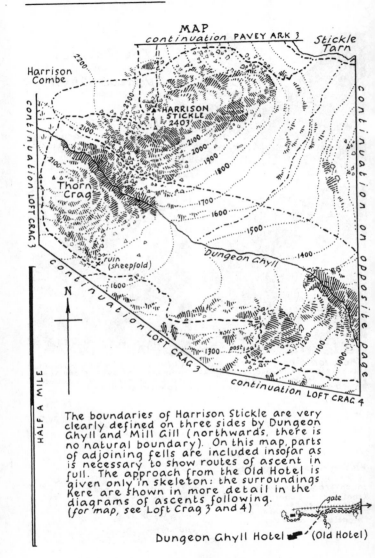

MAP
continuation PAVEY ARK 3 · Stickle Tarn

Harrison Combe

continuation LOFT CRAG 3

continuation LOFT CRAG 3

continuation on opposite page

HARRISON STICKLE 2403

Thorn Crag

ruin (sheepfold)

Dungeon Ghyll

2200

2100

2100

2100

2000

1900

1800

1700

1600

1500

1400

1600

1300

1200

1100

1000

post

N

HALF A MILE

continuation LOFT CRAG 4

The boundaries of Harrison Stickle are very clearly defined on three sides by Dungeon Ghyll and Mill Gill (northwards, there is no natural boundary). On this map, parts of adjoining fells are included insofar as is necessary to show routes of ascent in full. The approach from the Old Hotel is given only in skeleton: the surroundings here are shown in more detail in the diagrams of ascents following.
(for map, see Loft Crag 3 and 4)

gate

Dungeon Ghyll Hotel ⬛ (Old Hotel)

MAP

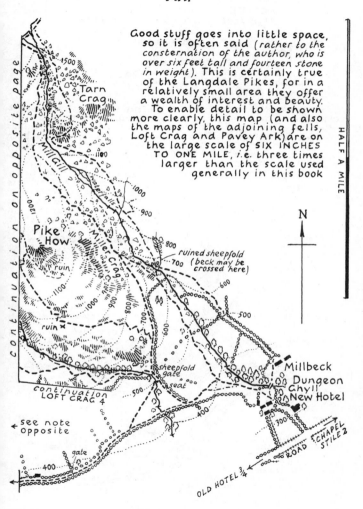

Good stuff goes into little space, so it is often said (rather to the consternation of the author, who is over six feet tall and fourteen stone in weight). This is certainly true of the Langdale Pikes, for in a relatively small area they offer a wealth of interest and beauty.

To enable detail to be shown more clearly, this map (and also the maps of the adjoining fells, Loft Crag and Pavey Ark) are on the large scale of SIX INCHES TO ONE MILE, i.e. three times larger than the scale used generally in this book

HALF A MILE

N

Tarn Crag

MILGILL

Pike How

ruin

Mill Crag

Waterfalls

ruined sheepfold (beck may be crossed here)

ruin ×

sheepfold
gate
seat

continuation on opposite page

continuation LOFT CRAG 4

← see note opposite

Millbeck
Dungeon
Ghyll
New Hotel

gate

ROAD

CHAPEL STILE 2

OLD HOTEL ¾

ASCENT FROM DUNGEON GHYLL
ROUTE 1 : *via* THORN CRAG
2150 feet of ascent : 2 miles

HARRISON STICKLE

THUNACAR KNOTT

Harrison Combe

grass

PIKE O' STICKLE

LOFT CRAG

2100

2100

2000

1900

1800

1700

Thorn Crag

x sheepfold (ruins)

GIMMER CRAG (a worth-while short detour on a level and easy path)

1600

grassy plateau

ROUTES 2 and 3

Dungeon Ghyll

summit fully in view

view down Middlefell Gully to Old Hotel

1500

1400

1300

1200

1100

1000

900

800

post

post

1700

1600

ROUTE 2

bracken

bracken

Pike How

summit comes into view

Middlefell Buttress

Raven Crag

900

Dungeon Ghyll Force

ROUTES 3 and 4

Dungeon Ghyll Hotel (Old Hotel)

gate

gate

500

gate and sheepfold

seat

ROUTE 4

400

Dungeon Ghyll New Hotel

looking north-west

ROAD

double bridge

300

Great Langdale Beck

CHAPEL STILE 2

This is the usual route, a very popular one, and every turn and twist of the ingenious and circuitous path has been faithfully followed by many generations of walkers. It is full of interest until the plateau below Thorn Crag is reached; thereafter, less so. It is rather remarkable that this route should have won preference over that *via* Pike How (Route 3), which is direct, much quicker, easier and better underfoot, while being no less attractive.

The similarity in the names of the two hotels is a source of confusion. The *Dungeon Ghyll Hotel*, three-quarters of a mile higher in the valley than the *New Hotel, Dungeon Ghyll* is now commonly, but not quite correctly, referred to as the *Old Hotel* (or, amongst the climbing fraternity, as 'Sid Cross's place').

ASCENT FROM DUNGEON GHYLL
ROUTE 2 : via THE DUNGEON GHYLL RAVINES
2150 feet of ascent : 1¾ miles

HARRISON STICKLE

THUNACAR KNOTT

Harrison Combe

PIKE O' STICKLE

ROUTE 1

grass

2100'

This is an adventurous route, unfrequented and pathless in the ravines, and involving some easy but steep scrambling in impressive surroundings.

Fourth Obstacle — a waterslide (insurmountable) between narrow rock walls. There is no escape from the ravine at this point. Retreat 150 yards to easier slope; or avoid ravine entirely by slanting across to join Route 3 lower down. The walls of this final ravine are dirty, loose, in an advanced state of decay, and unsafe. The ravine is subject to bombardment by scree spilling into it from the steep loose slope above; indeed, there is a risk of being brained by a shower of axes. (See notes for Route 3)

1700'   grass   STICKLE TARN

1500'

1400'

ROUTE 3

This waterfall almost unknown and rarely seen, is certainly one of the most attractive in Lakeland.

Third Obstacle — a beautiful 50' waterfall ends the ravine. Exit up steep rib (or gully) on left.

Second Obstacle — a choke of big boulders (shelter) through which, by trial and error, a way may be found free of difficulty.

First Obstacle — a 40' cascade avoided by steep slope on left.

ROUTE 1

1100'

900'

bracken

800'

summit comes into view

Middlefell Buttress

Raven Crag

Dungeon Ghyll Hotel (Old Hotel)

gate

gate

Dungeon Ghyll Force

ROUTES 3 and 4

500'

gate seat

ROUTE 4

400'

looking north-west

ROAD

300'

Dungeon Ghyll New Hotel

double bridge

Great Langdale Beck

CHAPEL STILE 2

BOTANISTS! — The sheltered recesses of the ravines harbour many varieties of flowers and ferns and other plants.

GHYLL or GILL? Properly GILL, according to the best authorities. GHYLL is a poetical affectation: it is too well established at Dungeon Ghyll to be altered now, and is accepted in a few other cases, e.g. Stock Ghyll, Ambleside.

ASCENT FROM DUNGEON GHYLL
ROUTE 3 : via PIKE HOW
2100 feet of ascent : 1½ miles

HARRISON STICKLE

THUNACAR KNOTT

Harrison Combe

grass

PIKE O' STICKLE

ROUTE 3

This steep scree slope above the ravine is loose. Except for the path, nothing is firm. This is the recently-discovered site of a prehistoric stone-axe 'factory' and much of the scree is the debris from working the stone and not the result of the weathering of the crags above.

1800
1700
grass
1600
1500

STICKLE TARN

Visitors to Langdale who do not know this route are urged to make its acquaintance. It is not only the quickest and easiest way to the top but has two other distinct virtues: first, it is pleasant underfoot, which is more than can be said for many Langdale paths, and, secondly, it is the 'purest' route, being a direct climb which does not encroach upon neighbouring fells.

bracken
1200

Pike How – a splendid viewpoint

1100
×ruin

Miller Crag

bracken

bracken

1000

bracken

ruin

ROUTES 1 and 2

Middlefell Buttress

Raven Crag

800

700

ROUTE 4

Dungeon Ghyll Force

Dungeon Ghyll Hotel (Old Hotel) →

gate

gate

500

600

gate and sheepfold
seat

ROUTE 4

looking north-west

400

Dungeon Ghyll New Hotel

300

ROAD

The rough lane along which the path runs from the Old Hotel was the main thoroughfare along the valley before the road was constructed and the hotels opened. A century ago the only place of refreshment hereabouts was Millbeck Farm, and the lane led directly to it from Mickleden. It can still be traced throughout its length but one of its enclosing walls has been allowed to crumble away.

double bridge

Great Langdale Beck

CHAPEL STILE 2

ASCENT FROM DUNGEON GHYLL
ROUTE 4 : via STICKLE TARN
2100 feet of ascent :
1¾ miles from the New Hotel ; 2¼ from the Old Hotel

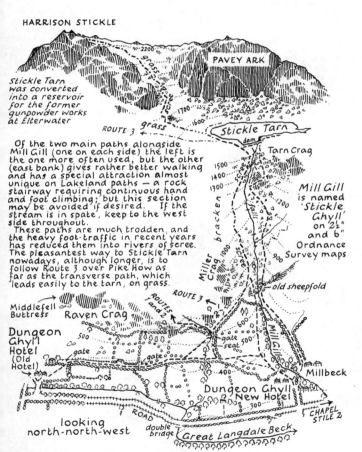

HARRISON STICKLE

PAVEY ARK

Stickle Tarn was converted into a reservoir for the former gunpowder works at Elterwater

ROUTE 3

grass

Stickle Tarn

dam

Tarn Crag

Mill Gill is named 'Stickle Ghyll' on 2½" and 6" Ordnance Survey maps

Of the two main paths alongside Mill Gill (one on each side) the left is the one more often used, but the other (east bank) gives rather better walking and has a special attraction almost unique on Lakeland paths — a rock stairway requiring continuous hand and foot climbing; but this section may be avoided if desired.   If the stream is in spate, keep to the west side throughout.

These paths are much trodden, and the heavy foot-traffic in recent years has reduced them into rivers of scree. The pleasantest way to Stickle Tarn nowadays, although longer, is to follow Route 3 over Pike How as far as the transverse path, which leads easily to the tarn, on grass.

old sheepfold

ROUTE 3

ROUTES 1 and 2

Middlefell Buttress

Raven Crag

gate   seat

gate

Dungeon Ghyll Hotel (Old Hotel)

gate

Millbeck

Dungeon Ghyll New Hotel

CHAPEL STILE 2

looking north-north-west

ROAD

double bridge

Great Langdale Beck

The highlight of this route is the impressive view of Pavey Ark, one of the finest scenes in Lakeland

ASCENTS FROM BORROWDALE AND GRASMERE

Harrison Stickle is remote from Borrowdale and Grasmere although not too distant to be reached, and the return made, in a day's walk.

All *natural* lines of ascent pass over intervening summits.

From BORROWDALE, either (i) first climb High Raise by the Greenup Edge path, or (ii) Pike o' Stickle by way of Langstrath and Stake Pass, in both cases then adopting the ridge routes from those summits. The alternative should be used for return.

From GRASMERE, either (i) first climb Sergeant Man, or (ii) Blea Rigg, descending from the latter to Stickle Tarn, whence the ascent may be completed.

Direct ascents *could* be worked out to avoid traversing other fells, but these would be artificial, probably no easier, and less interesting.

The fells mentioned above have separate chapters in this book, containing diagrams of ascent.

*The summit
from
Pike How*

*The summit
from
Stickle Tarn*

THE SUMMIT

The summit is an elevated ridge, 70 yards long and relatively narrow, falling away very sharply in crags at both ends. The main cairn is built on a rocky platform at the northern end and there is another, slightly lower, occupying the southern extremity above the precipitous Langdale face. A scanty covering of turf barely conceals the solid rock that here is very near the surface. The loftiness of the ridge and its commanding position endow a distinction to the summit that might be expected from its noble appearance in distant views.

DESCENTS (to Dungeon Ghyll):

With such a variety of attractive routes available, it would be a pity not to use an alternative to the one adopted for ascent (but Route 2 is less satisfactory as a way down, and needs care). The Pike How route is the easiest (most grass, least scree) and much the quickest. It should be obvious that direct descents from the south cairn are impracticable, but the warning must be given. Similarly, the tempting ridge leading straight down from the top towards Stickle Tarn is defended at its base by an almost continuous wall of crags : a scree gully going down from it on the left side is often used but is unpleasantly loose. Indeed, nothing but hard labour and trouble is to be gained by attempting descents that are independent of the regular paths.

THUNACAR KNOTT

PAVEY ARK (for DUNGEON GHYLL via Stickle Tarn (Route 4) bear to the right, downhill after 150 yards)

DUNGEON GHYLL (Routes 1, 2, 3)

grass shelf

N

100 YARDS

south cairn

THE VIEW

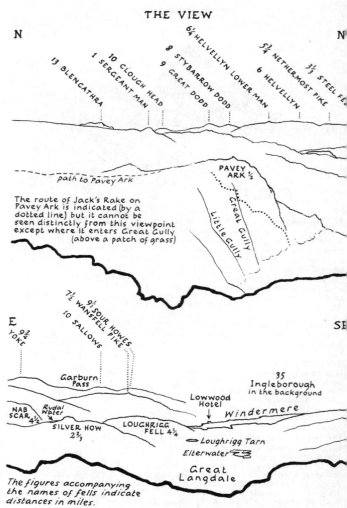

N

N

13 BLENCATHRA
1 SERGEANT MAN
10 CLOUGH HEAD
8 STYBARROW DODD
9 GREAT DODD
6¾ HELVELLYN LOWER MAN
5¾ NETHERMOST PIKE
6 HELVELLYN
3⅓ STEEL FE

path to Pavey Ark

PAVEY
ARK ½

The route of Jack's Rake on
Pavey Ark is indicated (by a
dotted line) but it cannot be
seen distinctly from this viewpoint
except where it enters Great Gully
(above a patch of grass)

Great Gully
Little Gully

E

9¾
YOKE

7½ SOUR HOWES
9½ WANSFELL PIKE
10 SALLOWS

SE

Garburn
Pass

35
Ingleborough
in the background

NAB
SCAR 4½
Rydal
Water

Lowwood
Hotel

Windermere

SILVER HOW
2⅔

LOUGHRIGG
FELL 4¼

→ Loughrigg Tarn

Elterwater

Great
Langdale

The figures accompanying
the names of fells indicate
distances in miles.

The thick line marks the visible boundaries
of the summit from the main cairn

THE VIEW

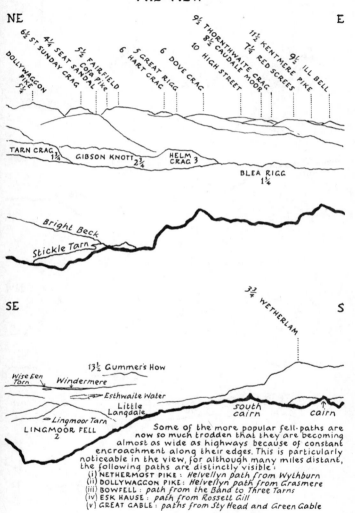

NE

E

DOLLYWAGGON PIKE 5¼
6½ ST SUNDAY CRAG
4¼ SEAT SANDAL
5½ COFA PIKE
FAIRFIELD
6 GREAT RIGG
5 HART CRAG
6 DOVE CRAG
10 HIGH STREET
9½ THORNTHWAITE CRAG
8¼ CAUDALE MOOR
7¼ RED SCREES
11½ KENTMERE PIKE
9½ ILL BELL

TARN CRAG 1¼
GIBSON KNOTT 2¾
HELM CRAG 3
BLEA RIGG 1¼

Bright Beck

Stickle Tarn

SE

S

3¾ WETHERLAM

13½ Gummer's How

Wise Een Tarn
Windermere
Esthwaite Water
Little Langdale
south cairn
cairn

Lingmoor Tarn
LINGMOOR FELL 2

Some of the more popular fell-paths are now so much trodden that they are becoming almost as wide as highways because of constant encroachment along their edges. This is particularly noticeable in the view, for although many miles distant, the following paths are distinctly visible:

(i) NETHERMOST PIKE : *Helvellyn path from Wythburn*
(ii) DOLLYWAGGON PIKE : *Helvellyn path from Grasmere*
(iii) BOWFELL : *path from the Band to Three Tarns*
(iv) ESK HAUSE : *path from Rossett Gill*
(v) GREAT GABLE : *paths from Sty Head and Green Gable*

THE VIEW

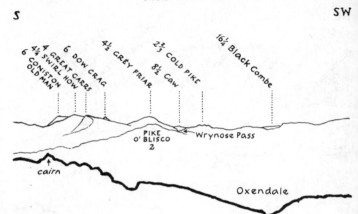

S   SW

6 CONISTON OLD MAN   4¼ SWIRL HOW   4 GREAT CARRS   6 DOW CRAG   4½ GREY FRIAR   2¾ COLD PIKE   8½ Caw   16¼ Black Combe

PIKE O' BLISCO 2   Wrynose Pass

cairn

Oxendale

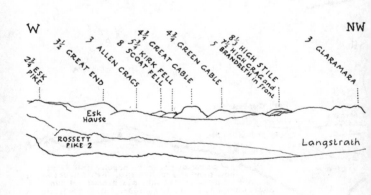

W   NW

2¾ ESK PIKE   3½ GREAT END   3 ALLEN CRAGS   8 SCOAT FELL   5¾ KIRK FELL   4¾ GREAT GABLE   4¾ GREEN GABLE   8½ HIGH STILE   7¾ HIGH CRAG and BRANDRETH in front   5   3 GLARAMARA

Esk Hause

ROSSETT PIKE 2   Langstrath

Harrison Combe

THE VIEW

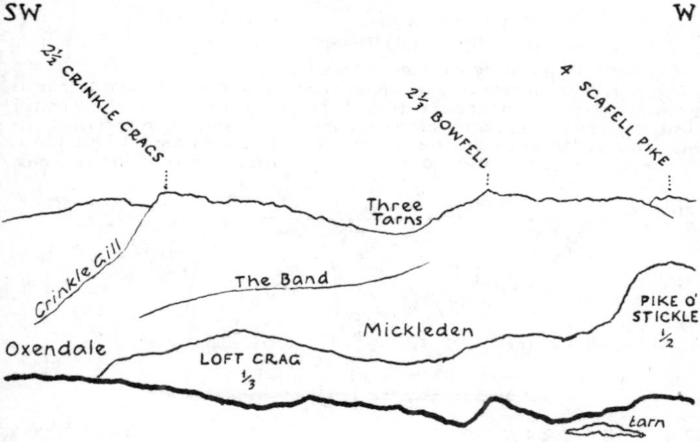
SW
W
2½ CRINKLE CRAGS
2⅓ BOWFELL
4 SCAFELL PIKE
Three Tarns
Crinkle Gill
The Band
PIKE O' STICKLE ½
Mickleden
Oxendale
LOFT CRAG ⅓
tarn

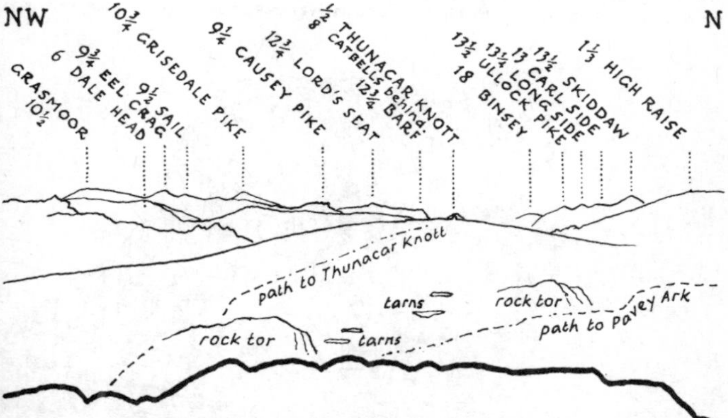
NW
N
GRASMOOR 10½
6 DALE HEAD
9¾ EEL CRAG
9½ SAIL
10¾ GRISEDALE PIKE
9¼ CAUSEY PIKE
12¾ LORD'S SEAT
8½ THUNACAR KNOTT
CATBELLS behind
12¼ BARF
18 BINSEY
13½ ULLOCK PIKE
13¼ LONG SIDE
13 CARL SIDE
13½ SKIDDAW
1⅓ HIGH RAISE
path to Thunacar Knott
tarns
rock tor
rock tor
tarns
path to Pavey Ark

Do not omit a visit to the south cairn, which has a striking downward view of Great Langdale. Stickle Tarn is better seen from here, and Blea Tarn comes into the picture. This is a particularly good viewpoint.

RIDGE ROUTES

TO PIKE O' STICKLE, 2323': ½ mile : W
Depression at 2075' : 250 feet of ascent
An easy walk, ending with an enjoyable scramble

The objective is clearly in view and its distinctive outline is unmistakable. The route is direct (it 'short-cuts' the ridge) and is easily traced in clear weather, although indistinct in marshy ground near the crossing of the stream. The final scramble is steep and rocky, and permits of minor variations.

TO LOFT CRAG, 2270': ⅓ mile : W, then S and W
Depression at 2070' : 200 feet of ascent
An easy walk, with a fine little summit at the finish

Loft Crag is the biggest eminence on the ridge to the left of Pike o' Stickle. Take the usual route for Langdale (Route 1), turning off right at the Thorn Crag col along a narrow track and then left up a small but prominent scree-run to the ridge.

Harrison Stickle from Loft Crag

RIDGE ROUTES

To THUNACAR KNOTT, 2351' : ½ mile · NNW
Depression at 2225': 140 feet of ascent
A dull trudge from the spectacular to the uninteresting.

The path starts distinctly from the main cairn but beyond the rock tor becomes obscure in a depression : here follow the line of cairns leading half-left to an improving path (another track develops from a line of cairns going straight on, but loses itself amongst the boulders ahead). The recognised top of Thunacar Knott is marked by a big cairn beyond a tarn, although higher ground is crossed on the way to it. The path keeps to the right and goes on to High Raise.

To PAVEY ARK, 2288'
½ mile : N, then NE
Depression at 2225'
100 feet of ascent
An interesting path

Although not strictly a ridge route, this is a popular walk. From the main cairn, descend the steep but easy rocks directly below to join a good path, much of it over bare rock, linking the two summits. Anyone who does not like the look of the initial descent may avoid it by taking the Thunacar Knott route at the start and slanting across to the Pavey Ark path over grass on the near side of the rock tor.

HALF A MILE

Pavey Ark from the path

top of Jack's Rake

pinnacle

Helm Crag

1299'

affectionately known as
'The Lion and The Lamb'

HELM CRAG ▲

Grasmere ●

MILES

0 1 2

from Grasmere

This is the smallest (and most accurate!) map in the book

NATURAL FEATURES

Helm Crag may well be the best-known of all Lakeland fells, and possibly even the best-known hill in the country. Generations of waggonette and motor-coach tourists have been tutored to recognise its appearance in the Grasmere landscape : it is the one feature of their Lakeland tour they hail at sight, and in unison, but the cry on their lips is not "Helm Crag!" but "The Lion and the Lamb!" — in a variety of dialects. The resemblance of the summit rocks to a lion is so striking that recognition, from several viewpoints, is instant ; yet, oddly, the outline most like Leo is not the official 'Lion' at all : in fact there are two lions, each with a lamb, and each guards one end of the summit ridge as though set there by architectural design. The summit is altogether a rather weird and fantastic place, well worth not merely a visit but a detailed and leisurely exploration. Indeed the whole fell, although of small extent, is unusually interesting; its very appearance is challenging; its sides are steep, rough and craggy; its top bristles ; it *looks* irascible, like a shaggy terrier in a company of sleek foxhounds, for all around are loftier and smoother fells, circling the pleasant vale of Grasmere out of which Helm Crag rises so abruptly.

The fell is not isolated, nor independent of others, for it is the termination of a long ridge enclosing Far Easedale in a graceful curve on north and east and rising, finally, to the rocky peak of Calf Crag. It drains quickly, is dry underfoot, and has no streams worthy of mention.

The virtues of Helm Crag have not been lauded enough. It gives an exhilarating little climb, a brief essay in real mountaineering, and, in a region where all is beautiful, it makes a notable contribution to the natural charms and attractions of Grasmere.

outline of
STEEL FELL

DUNMAIL
RAISE

THE
GREENBURN
VALLEY

summit
scene

MAP

N

continuation
GIBSON KNOTT 2

GREENBURN VALLEY

TOWN HEAD

Far Easedale

BORROWDALE

stepping stones (Stythwaite Steps)

Far Easedale Gill

Easedale Gill

Gill Foot

Low Mill Bridge

TRAVELLERS REST

HELM CRAG 1299

Brimmer Head Beck

Kitty Crag

EASEDALE TARN

River Rothay

KESWICK

YH

Easedale

ONE MILE

Note that the scale of this map is larger than that commonly used in this book

Goody Bridge

Butharlyp (Butterlip) How

SILVER HOW

LANGDALE

Grasmere

AMBLESIDE

The summit rocks from the north.

ASCENT FROM GRASMERE
1100 feet of ascent : 1½ miles
HELM CRAG

This is one of the few hills where ascent and descent by the same route is recommended, the popular path depicted being much the best way both up and down. An alternative route (shown on the map but not on this diagram) has nothing in its favour.

If, however, Helm Crag is to be a part only of the day's programme (e.g. the circuit of Far Easedale or the Greenburn valley) it is better reserved for descent, for then the Vale of Grasmere will be directly in view ahead; and this fair scene is at its best when the shadows of evening are lengthening, with the Langdales silhouetted in rugged outline against the sunset. Tarry long over this exquisite picture of serenity and peace, and memorise it for the long winter of exile!

looking north-west

This is a splendid little climb; if it has a fault it is that it is too short. But for the evening of the day of arrival in Grasmere on a walking holiday it is just the thing : an epitome of Lakeland concentrated in the space of two hours — and an excellent foretaste of happy days to come.

THE SUMMIT

Rocks at the north-west end of the summit ridge, *known by various names:*
(a) The 'Lion Couchant, *or, more popularly,* The Lion and The Lamb, *(as seen from the road below Dunmail Raise)*
(b) The Howitzer *(as seen from Dunmail Raise)*

The highest point of the rocks is the true summit of the fell

In scenic values, the summits of many high mountains are a disappointment after the long toil of ascent, yet here, on the top of little Helm Crag, a midget of a mountain, is a remarkable array of rocks, upstanding and fallen, of singular interest and fascinating appearance, that yield a quality of reward out of all proportion to the short and simple climb. The uppermost inches of Scafell and Helvellyn and Skiddaw can show nothing like Helm Crag's crown of shattered and petrified stone : indeed, its highest point, a pinnacle of rock airily thrust out above a dark abyss, is not to be attained by walking and is brought underfoot only by precarious manœuvres of the body. This is one of the very few summits in Lakeland reached only by climbing rocks, and it is certainly (but not for that reason alone) one of the very best.

continued

THE SUMMIT

continued

The summit ridge is 250 yards in length and is adorned at each end by fangs of rock overtopping the fairly level path. Between these towers there have been others in ages past but all that remains of them now is a chaos of collapsed boulders, choking a strange depression that extends the full length of the summit on the north-east side. The depression is bounded by a secondary ridge, and this in turn descends craggily to an even more strange depression, in appearance resembling a huge ditch cleft straight as a furrow across the breast of the fell for 300 yards; or, more romantically, a deep moat defending the turreted wall of the castle above. This surprising feature, which will not be seen unless searched for, will doubtless be readily explained by geologists (or antiquaries?); to the unlearned beholder it seems likely to be the result of some ancient natural convulsion that caused the side of the fell to slip downwards a few yards before coming to rest. This ditch is also bounded on its far side by a parallel ridge or parapet (narrow, and an interesting walk) beyond which the fellside plunges down almost precipitously to the valley, falling in juniper-clad crags.

Care is necessary when exploring the boulder-strewn depressions on the summit, especially if the rocks are greasy. There are many good natural shelters here, and some dangerous clefts and fissures and holes, so well protected from the weather that summer flowers are to be found in bloom in their recesses as late as mid-winter.

The south-west side of the summit ridge consists mainly of bracken slopes and are of little interest in their upper reaches.

DESCENTS : Always use the ridge-path for descent to Grasmere. Watch for the zig-zag turning down left from the ridge, especially in mist, and ignore the misleading green path going straight on : this ends above crags.

THE SUMMIT

Rocks at the north-west end of the summit-ridge known as **The Old Woman Playing the Organ** *from their appearance when seen from Tongue Gill and the vicinity of Easedale Tarn*

Rocks at the south-east end of the summit-ridge. *These form the OFFICIAL* **Lion and The Lamb** *(as seen from the Swan Hotel, Grasmere). The lion's head is the O.S. 'station' (altitude 1299') but is not quite the highest point of the fell*

THE VIEW

This is the view from the cairn on the summit ridge — whether it coincides with the view from the highest point the author will never know for his several attempts to mount to the rocky pate of the Lion Couchant have all been defeated by a lack of resolution; but probably it is the same. In any case, most visitors will be content to study the prospect from the comparative security of the cairn on the ridge.

continued

continued

The Vale of Grasmere is best displayed from the head of the other (official) Lion, which even the author found a simple ascent, (although deeply conscious of precipices all around).

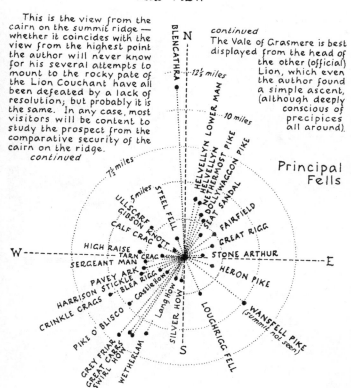

Principal Fells

The prominent height south-south-east (to the right of Loughrigg Fell) is Gummers How, 13 miles distant at the foot of Windermere.

This corner was reserved for an announcement that the author had succeeded in surmounting the highest point. Up to the time of going to press, however, such an announcement cannot be made.

Lakes and Tarns

SE: *Windermere (upper reach)*
SSE: *Grasmere*
SSE: *Esthwaite Water*
WSW: *Easedale Tarn*

Tarn Crag
across Far Easedale
from the slopes of Helm Crag

The north-east face
from Low Mill Bridge

RIDGE ROUTE

To GIBSON KNOTT, 1379'
   1 mile : NW, then W
   Depression at 1050'
   400 feet of ascent
   An interesting ridge climb

Two big cairns indicate the way off
Helm Crag. A narrow path crosses the
depression and continues up the opposite
slope; when it starts to traverse the face
leave it and keep to the ridge, where another
track winds charmingly between rock outcrops.
The cairned summit rises across a shallow hollow.

ONE MILE

Helm Crag, from the path to Gibson Knott

High Raise

**summit named
High White Stones**

2500'

*from Great Crag,
Watendlath Fell*

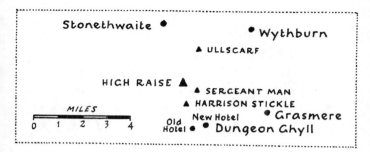

NATURAL FEATURES

It is usual to regard High Raise as Lakeland's most centrally situated fell. An area without definite boundaries cannot have a determinable centre, and the 'most central fell' must remain a matter of individual opinion. A study of the map of the district suggests that High Raise has a decided bias to the south, however, and that Ullscarf better fits the description, while, a little further north, Armboth Fell seems even more deserving of the title. The most that can be said of High Raise, with certainty, is that its summit is the maximum elevation of the central axis or watershed. Hereabouts the surround of mountainous country is complete, the western arc being occupied by a tumultuous skyline and the eastern horizon formed of lofty, smooth ranges; but, quite obviously, the viewpoint is dwarfed in altitude by many summits in this fine panorama. Nevertheless, High Raise occupies a magnificent position geographically, many valleys radiating from the wide upper slopes. The fell's attractions, except as a viewpoint and an easy promenade, are limited, distinctive natural features being absent from the rounded grassy slopes — remarkably so when one considers how full of character are the subsidiary summits of the main mass overlooking Great Langdale and Langstrath. Drainage is provided by these two valleys, Langstrath taking away most of the water, with the assistance of Greenup Gill and Wyth Burn in the north.

MAP

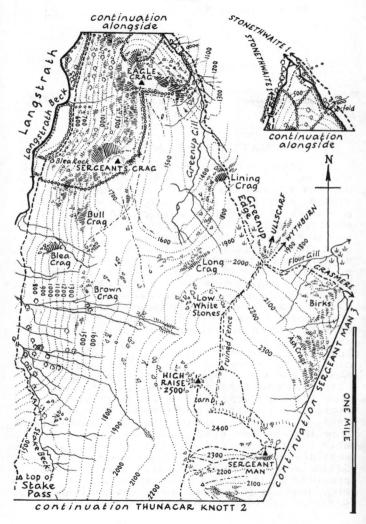

ASCENT FROM DUNGEON GHYLL
2250 feet of ascent : 2½ miles from the New Hotel

looking north-west

HIGH RAISE

grass 2400

2300 } SERGEANT MAN

THUNACAR KNOTT
and HARRISON STICKLE

2200

good small wind-shelter
in cluster of grey rocks

Bright Beck —
the top of the ravine

2100
2000
1900
1800

When the path fades away, the
best plan is to get in the bed
of the gill and follow it to
its source. It is never too
rough to negotiate, and
the beck leaves ample
room for pedestrian
perambulations.

Bright Beck

1700

PAVEY ARK
(via North Rake)

HARRISON
STICKLE

PAVEY
ARK

1600

Stickle Tarn
dam

SERGEANT MAN
and BLEA RIGG

1500
1400

Mill Gill

DUNGEON GHYLL

For details of the paths to Stickle Tarn
see Harrison Stickle 10

Looking from Stickle Tarn, the route is
hidden and unsuspected, the upper reach
of Bright Beck being screened by the bulk
of Pavey Ark, which is omitted, for clarity,
from the diagram, although, in fact, it is the
most striking object seen on the journey.

The route illustrated is the only practicable direct way
to High Raise from Dungeon Ghyll that does not involve the
climbing of intermediate summits. It has much to commend
it as a quick, easy and foolproof way to the top, for beyond
Stickle Tarn the gradients are surprisingly gentle while the
route is closely defined by Bright Beck, but it can hardly be
described as interesting, and, if time and extra effort are
of no consequence, the best way to High Raise from the south
will always lie over the top of Harrison Stickle.

ASCENT FROM GRASMERE
2350 feet of ascent : 5½ miles

HIGH RAISE — Low White Stones

Turn left alongside old fence when Greenup is reached. (Path ahead goes to Borrowdale)

2400 — ruined fence — 2300 — 2200 — 2100 — Greenup Edge — ULLSCARF

path dodges from one side of the fence to the other to avoid wet ground

2000 — 2000 — Ash Crags — 1900 — 1800 — 1700

SERGEANT MAN

Wyth Burn — WYTHBURN

The first fence reached marks the head of Far Easedale, NOT Greenup. Go straight on here. This is a confusing place in mist.

ruined fence

Ferngill Crag — stile — fold × — CALF CRAG

Ferngill — CALF CRAG

Moor Moss — 1600 — 1500 — 1400 — 1300

Recent generations of walkers have blazed a new trail to the head of Far Easedale. Originally, the bridle-path crossed the beck half-a-mile lower down, but it cannot now be traced on the ground although still shown on some maps in current use to the exclusion of the new track.

path crosses slab above fall, and needs care — 1200 — waterfall — cascades × sheepfold

The shapely peak here is Pike of Carrs

Far Easedale — tarned path — Carrs Gill — Horn Crag

Deer Bield Crag (vertical grey rock)

sheepfold (ruins) — ×waterfall

1000 — 900 — 800

×waterfall — 700 — 600 — ×waterfall — ×sheepfold

If the return is to be made to Grasmere, and the weather is clear, the alternative route via Sergeant Man (and then preferably Blea Rigg) is strongly recommended for the descent.

Stythwaite Steps (stepping stones)

This is an interesting route besides being direct, practicable in mist, and avoiding other summits; as far as Greenup Edge use is made of the path along Far Easedale to Borrowdale.

500

GRASMERE 2

For details of the route to Stythwaite Steps, see map Helm Crag 3

looking west-north-west

ASCENT FROM WYTHBURN
1950 feet of ascent : 5 miles from Wythburn Church

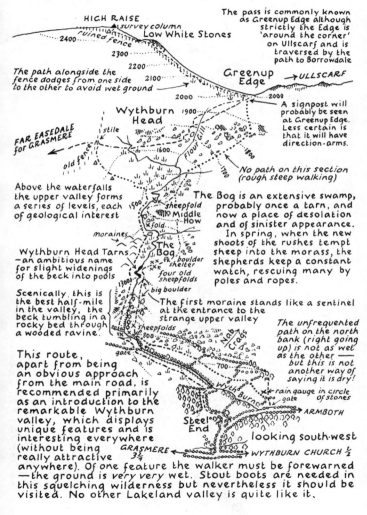

The pass is commonly known as Greenup Edge although strictly the Edge is 'around the corner' on Ullscarf and is traversed by the path to Borrowdale

HIGH RAISE
survey column
ruined fence
Low White Stones
2400
2300
2200
2100
Greenup Edge → ULLSCARF
The path alongside the fence dodges from one side to the other to avoid wet ground
2000
A signpost will probably be seen at Greenup Edge. Less certain is that it will have direction-arms.

Wythburn Head
1900
FAR EASEDALE for GRASMERE
stile
1600
No path on this section (rough steep walking)
old fence

Above the waterfalls the upper valley forms a series of levels, each of geological interest
1500
sheepfold
Middle How fold
moraines
The Bog is an extensive swamp, probably once a tarn, and now a place of desolation and of sinister appearance. In spring, when the new shoots of the rushes tempt sheep into the morass, the shepherds keep a constant watch, rescuing many by poles and ropes.

Wythburn Head Tarns —an ambitious name for slight widenings of the beck into pools
The Bog
boulder shelter
four old sheepfolds
big boulder

Scenically this is the best half-mile in the valley, the beck tumbling in a rocky bed through a wooded ravine.
The first moraine stands like a sentinel at the entrance to the strange upper valley

The unfrequented path on the north bank (right going up) is not as wet as the other — but this is not another way of saying it is dry!
800
sheepfolds
Nab Crags
700

This route, apart from being an obvious approach from the main road, is recommended primarily as an introduction to the remarkable Wythburn valley, which displays unique features and is interesting everywhere (without being really attractive anywhere). Of one feature the walker must be forewarned —the ground is *very very* wet. Stout boots are needed in this squelching wilderness but nevertheless it should be visited. No other Lakeland valley is quite like it.
gate
Wythburn
rain gauge in circle of stones
gate
→ ARMBOTH
Steel End
looking south-west
GRASMERE 3¾ →
→ WYTHBURN CHURCH ½

ASCENT FROM STONETHWAITE
2200 feet of ascent · 3¾ miles

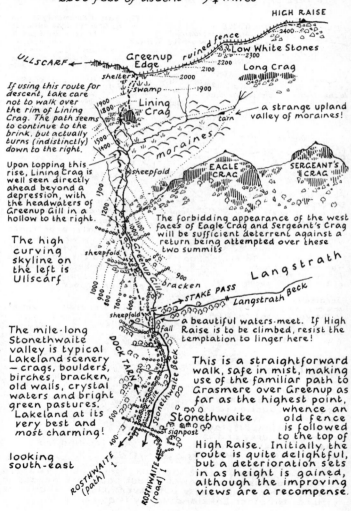

HIGH RAISE

ruined fence

2400

Low White Stones

2300

ULLSCARF ←

Greenup Edge

2200

Long Crag

2100

shelter

2000

swamp

1900

Lining Crag

1900
1800

a strange upland valley of moraines!

If using this route for descent, take care not to walk over the rim of Lining Crag. The path seems to continue to the brink, but actually turns (indistinctly) down to the right.

1500
1400

tarn

moraines

EAGLE CRAG

SERGEANT'S CRAG

Upon topping this rise, Lining Crag is well seen directly ahead beyond a depression, with the headwaters of Greenup Gill in a hollow to the right.

1700

sheepfold

The forbidding appearance of the west faces of Eagle Crag and Sergeant's Crag will be sufficient deterrent against a return being attempted over these two summits

The high curving skyline on the left is Ullscarf

1200

sheepfold

1000

Langstrath

900

bracken

→ STAKE PASS

Langstrath Beck

800

sheepfold

fall

a beautiful waters-meet. If High Raise is to be climbed, resist the temptation to linger here!

The mile-long Stonethwaite valley is typical Lakeland scenery — crags, boulders, birches, bracken, old walls, crystal waters and bright green pastures. Lakeland at its very best and most charming!

DOCK TARN

Stonethwaite Beck

500

This is a straightforward walk, safe in mist, making use of the familiar path to Grasmere over Greenup as far as the highest point, whence an old fence is followed to the top of High Raise. Initially, the route is quite delightful, but a deterioration sets in as height is gained, although the improving views are a recompense.

Stonethwaite

signpost

looking south-east

400

ROSTHWAITE (path) 1

ROSTHWAITE (road) 1

THE SUMMIT

High Raise is often wrongly referred to as High White Stones. High Raise is the name of the fell, High White Stones the name of a small area of grey boulders which includes the summit. All else is grass, a vast sheepwalk in the form of a broad plateau little different from a valley pasture except that here drains and irrigation channels are absent and there is much marshy ground. The big cairn, and an adjacent survey column, stand at the top of the Langstrath slope, 150 yards west of a ruined fence: on the line of this fence, north-east, is a second cairn that features prominently in many views of the fell. Walking across the top is everywhere very easy.

DESCENTS : The path for GREAT LANGDALE leaves the main cairn, and becomes clear after crossing the stones. *In bad weather*, there is a safe escape from the ridge (which may lead to difficulties nearer to Harrison Stickle) by slanting left to Bright Beck at the first depression; this goes down to Stickle Tarn.

FOR GREENUP (and BORROWDALE, GRASMERE or WYTHBURN) follow the old fence northwards from the second cairn. The descent to BORROWDALE *via* Sergeant's Crag is pathless, takes longer than the Greenup route, and is amongst crags; *in bad weather it should not be attempted.*

STAKE PASS is in view from the main cairn and may be reached

1: Greenup
2: Sergeant's Crag
3: Langdale and Harrison Stickle
4: Sergeant Man

by a beeline (no path) but it is easier to take advantage at first of the Langdale path, slanting off right at the depression. It is well to remember, if time is short, that Stake Pass is far distant from habitations, and that nothing is saved by a visit thereto.

THE VIEW

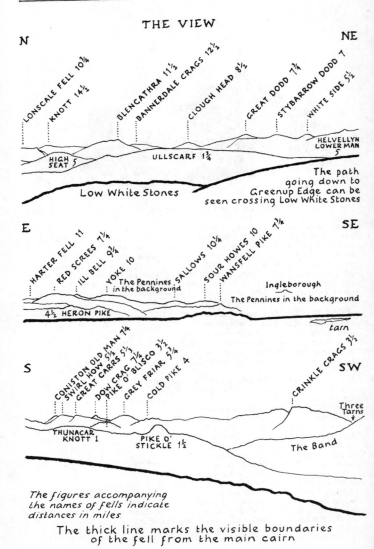

The figures accompanying
the names of fells indicate
distances in miles.

The thick line marks the visible boundaries
of the fell from the main cairn

THE VIEW

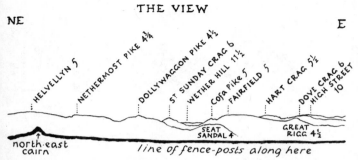

NE   E

HELVELLYN 5 • NETHERMOST PIKE 4¾ • DOLLYWAGGON PIKE 4½ • ST SUNDAY CRAG 6 • WETHER HILL 11½ • COFA PIKE 5 • FAIRFIELD 5 • HART CRAG 5½ • DOVE CRAG 6 • HIGH STREET 10

SEAT SANDAL 4   GREAT RIGG 4½

north-east cairn   *line of fence-posts along here*

New features, notably the Wythburn valley and the summit of Sergeant Man, are brought into view by a visit to the north-east cairn. The conspicuous path seen climbing the breast of Nethermost Pike is the Wythburn path to Helvellyn.

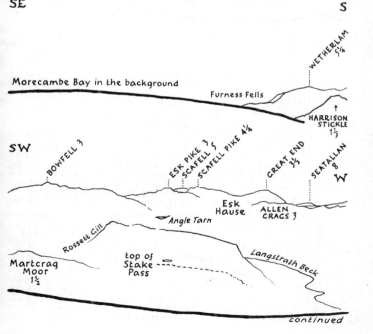

SE   S

WETHERLAM 5¼

Morecambe Bay in the background   Furness Fells

HARRISON STICKLE 1⅓

SW   W

BOWFELL 3   ESK PIKE 3 • SCAFELL 5 • SCAFELL PIKE 4¾   GREAT END 3½ • SEATALLAN 8

Esk Hause   ALLEN CRAGS 3

Angle Tarn

Rossett Gill

Martcrag Moor 1½   top of Stake Pass   Langstrath Beck

continued

THE VIEW

continued

W   NW

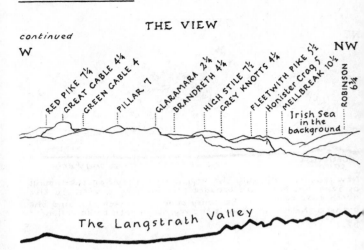

RED PIKE 7¼ GREAT GABLE 4¼ GREEN GABLE 4 PILLAR 7 GLARAMARA 2¼ BRANDRETH 4¼ HIGH STILE 7½ GREY KNOTTS 4¼ FLEETWITH PIKE 5½ HONISTER CRAG 5 MELLBREAK 10½ ROBINSON 6¾

Irish Sea
in the
background

The Langstrath Valley

RIDGE ROUTES

To THUNACAR KNOTT, 2351': 1 mile : S
Depression at 2225': 130 feet of ascent
An easy, straightforward walk

HIGH RAISE
survey × column

grass

broken fence

grass

2400

2300

2200

2200

2300

SERGEANT MAN

N

tarn ○ THUNACAR KNOTT

On the south side of the cairn a grassy path leaves the stones and goes easily down to cross a wide depression before climbing gently to Thunacar Knott, the summit-cairn being 60 yards west of the path. Ignore a distinct track branching left (to Pavey Ark) as the first stones of the Knott are reached

ONE MILE

To SERGEANT MAN, 2414':
½ mile : SE, then S
Depression at 2370': 60 feet of ascent
Merely a stroll

Sergeant Man cannot be seen from High Raise main cairn (although it is visible from the one north-east). Cross the top to the tarn and the old fence, where a path of sorts will be found.

THE VIEW

NW

N

DALE HEAD 5¼ 9½
GRASMOOR 6
HINDSCARTH 6
EEL CRAG 8¾
SAIL 8¼
GRISEDALE PIKE 9½
CAUSEY PIKE 8
BROOM FELL 12
LORD'S SEAT 11½
BARF 11½
ULLOCK PIKE 12
LONG SIDE 11½
CARL SIDE 11½
SKIDDAW 12

Solway Firth
in the background

Bassenthwaite
Lake

HIGH SPY
5

MAIDEN
MOOR
6

CATBELLS 7

Derwentwater

Tarn at Leaves

Borrowdale

GRANGE FELL
4¼

ROSTHWAITE
FELL 2½

SERGEANT'S
CRAG 1¼

EAGLE CRAG 1½

survey
column

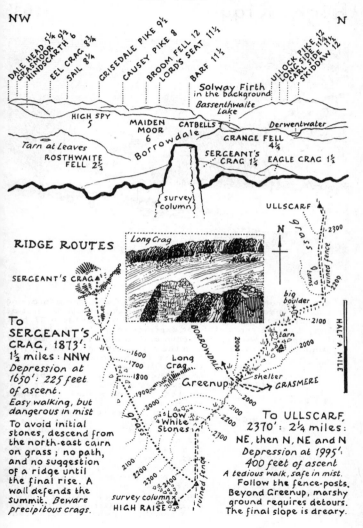

RIDGE ROUTES

Long Crag

ULLSCARF

2300

ruined fence

2200

SERGEANT'S CRAG

big
boulder

2100

HALF A MILE

2000

To
SERGEANT'S
CRAG, 1873':
1½ miles: NNW
*Depression at
1650': 225 feet
of ascent.*
Easy walking, but
dangerous in mist.

1600
1700
1800
1900

tarn

2000

shelter → GRASMERE

To avoid initial
stones, descend from
the north-east cairn
on grass; no path,
and no suggestion
of a ridge until
the final rise. A
wall defends the
summit. *Beware
precipitous crags.*

Long
Crag

BORROWDALE

Greenup

2000

2100

2200

Low
White
Stones

2300

To ULLSCARF,
2370': 2¼ miles:
NE, then N, NE and N
*Depression at 1995':
400 feet of ascent.*
A tedious walk, safe in mist.
Follow the fence-posts.
Beyond Greenup, marshy
ground requires detours.
The final slope is dreary.

2100

2200

2300

2400

survey column ×
HIGH RAISE ▲

ruined fence

High Rigg

from Sosgill Bridge

The valley running north from Dunmail Raise, and containing Thirlmere, is suddenly confronted by a steep, abrupt fell just at that final stage in its course when, with the highest hills left behind, it might reasonably be expected to go on more leisurely, as is the fashion with valleys born among mountains. Escape is found in a narrow ravine to the right, which opens out into St.John's-in-the-Vale; and, because this intrusive fell stands in isolation from other high ground, a subsidiary valley, that of Naddle Beck, forms at the base of the left flank. The waters mingle only when the River Greta is joined four miles to the north. This isolated wedge is High Rigg (locally known as Naddle Fell): it is rough and craggy although of modest elevation only. Northwards the ridge falls to a pass, where there is a Church, so sited to serve both valleys equally (and an object of pilgrimage for many visitors to Keswick), beyond which rises Low Rigg, merely a rough pasture, followed by an easy slope descending to Tewet Tarn and the Keswick-Penrith road.

Threlkeld ●

● Keswick

Dale ● ▲ HIGH RIGG
Bottom

Smaithwaite Bridge ●

MILES
0   1   2   3   4

MAP

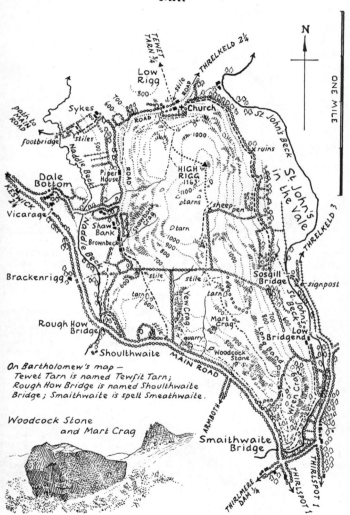

On Bartholomew's map —
Tewet Tarn is named Tewfit Tarn;
Rough How Bridge is named Shoulthwaite
Bridge; Smaithwaite is spelt Smeathwaite.

Woodcock Stone
and Mart Crag

ASCENT FROM THE CHURCH OF St JOHN'S-IN-THE-VALE
450 feet of ascent : ½ mile

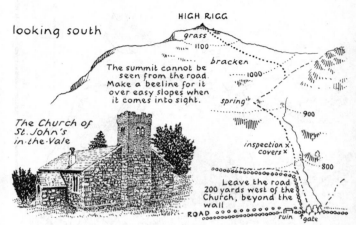

looking south

HIGH RIGG

grass

1100

bracken

1000

The summit cannot be seen from the road. Make a beeline for it over easy slopes when it comes into sight.

spring

900

The Church of St. John's in-the-Vale

inspection x covers x

800

Leave the road 200 yards west of the Church, beyond the wall

ROAD

ruin   gate

This short climb is as simple as the diagram suggests, although not appreciably helped by paths. Anybody full of the joy of Spring will do it in 15 minutes (author's time : 35 min.)

TRAVERSE OF THE RIDGE

The full traverse of the ridge, starting up the wooded slope from Smaithwaite Bridge and continuing over High Rigg and Low Rigg to Tewet Tarn and the Penrith road, is a splendid little expedition admirably suited to old and rickety fellwalkers long past their best. The journey should be made from south to north so that the fine view of Blencathra is in front. On a calm clear day this splendid mountain is perfectly mirrored in the waters of Tewet Tarn.

THE SUMMIT

GREAT CALVA

BLENCATHRA

Tewet Tarn

The cairn stands on a small rocky knoll, easily identifiable although not appreciably higher than some other parts of the fell.
The route of ascent should be reversed for descent : there are crags in all other directions.

THE VIEW

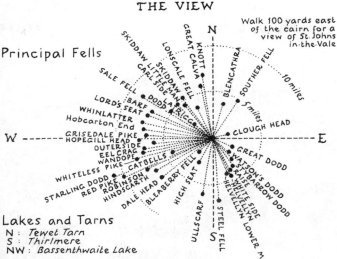

Principal Fells

Walk 100 yards east
of the cairn for a
view of St. Johns
in-the-Vale

Fells labelled (clockwise from N): GREAT CALVA, KNOTT, SKIDDAW LITTLE MAN, LONSCALE FELL, SKIDDAW, CARL SIDE, LAING, DODD, LATRIGG, BARF, LORD'S SEAT, WHINLATTER, Hobcarton End, GRISEDALE PIKE, HOPEGILL HEAD, OUTERSIDE, EEL CRAG, WANDOPE, WHITELESS PIKE, CATBELLS, STARLING DODD, RED PIKE, ROBINSON, HINDSCARTH, DALE HEAD, BLEABERRY FELL, HIGH SEAT, SALE FELL, BLENCATHRA, SOUTHER FELL, CLOUGH HEAD, GREAT DODD, WATSON'S DODD, STYBARROW DODD, RAISE, WHITE SIDE, HELVELLYN LOWER MAN, HELVELLYN, STEEL FELL, ULLSCARF

5 miles / 10 miles

Lakes and Tarns
N : *Tewet Tarn*
S : *Thirlmere*
NW : *Bassenthwaite Lake*

The view is interesting, with Blencathra
especially well displayed and Clough Head
very impressive. The isolated position of High Rigg in relation to the
other fells on or about the central ridge is emphasised by the sight
of Helvellyn to the *left* of its Lower Man and of Skiddaw to the *right*
of its Little Man. From all other central viewpoints the reverse obtains.

looking south to Helvellyn

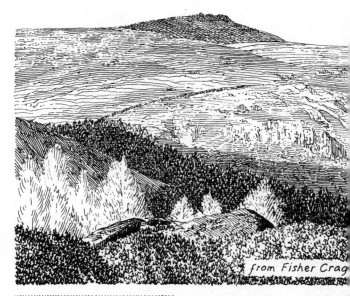

from Fisher Crag

Reecastle Crag

• Keswick

Dale Bottom

BLEABERRY
▲ FELL

• Lodore
▲ HIGH SEAT
• Armboth
▲ HIGH TOVE
•
Watendlath
• Rosthwaite

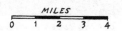

MILES

0   1   2   3   4

NATURAL FEATURES

High Seat is the principal fell on the north section of the central ridge, overtopping all others within a radius of some miles, and is, therefore, an excellent viewpoint. Its limits are well-defined by watercourses: Ashness Gill, Watendlath Beck and Raise Gill westwards and Mere Gill and Shoulthwaite Gill on the eastern flank. As with all the fells on the Thirlmere and Borrowdale watershed the top is uninteresting, and all the charm and excitement concentrates in the steep and craggy lower slopes, especially on those to the west above Derwentwater, where the woods of Lodore and Ashness are supremely lovely, crag and coppice and cascade combining to present scenes of peerless beauty. A curiosity on the eastern side is the great rock barrier of Raven Crag, which deflects all streams north to the narrow ravine of Shoulthwaite Gill and away from Thirlmere, for which they seem, at first, to be naturally destined.

As a climb, High Seat is less meritorious than its initial approaches and fine situation suggest, due partly to the extreme dreariness of the upper plateau, that not even a rich carpet of heather can dispel, but more particularly due to the universal swampiness of the ultimate slopes.

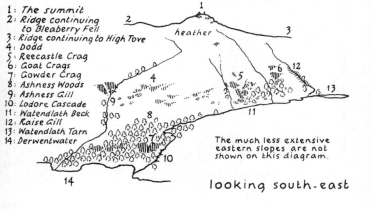

1 : The summit
2 : Ridge continuing to Bleaberry Fell
3 : Ridge continuing to High Tove
4 : Dodd
5 : Reecastle Crag
6 : Goat Crags
7 : Gowder Crag
8 : Ashness Woods
9 : Ashness Gill
10 : Lodore Cascade
11 : Watendlath Beck
12 : Raise Gill
13 : Watendlath Tarn
14 : Derwentwater

heather

The much less extensive eastern slopes are not shown on this diagram.

looking south-east

MAP

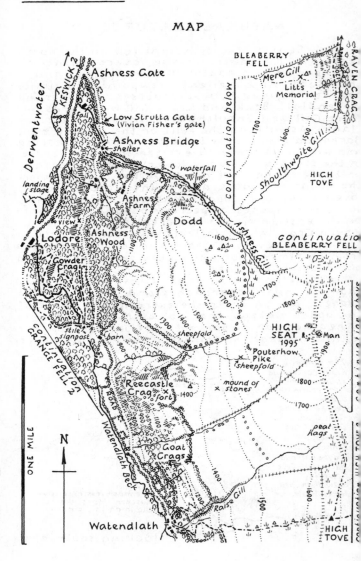

ASCENT FROM ASHNESS BRIDGE
1500 feet of ascent : 2 miles (4½ from Keswick)

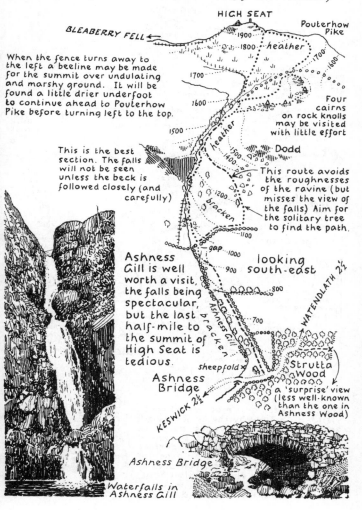

HIGH SEAT

Pouterhow Pike

BLEABERRY FELL ←

1900
1800 *heather*
1700
1600

When the fence turns away to the left a beeline may be made for the summit over undulating and marshy ground. It will be found a little drier underfoot to continue ahead to Pouterhow Pike before turning left to the top.

1700

1600

1500

Four cairns on rock knolls may be visited with little effort

heather

Dodd

This is the best section. The falls will not be seen unless the beck is followed closely (and carefully)

1500
1400

1200

bracken

This route avoids the roughnesses of the ravine (but misses the view of the falls) Aim for the solitary tree to find the path.

1100

gap — 1000

900

looking south-east

800

Ashness Gill is well worth a visit, the falls being spectacular, but the last half-mile to the summit of High Seat is tedious.

700

WATENDLATH 2½

Ashness Gill

bracken

Ashness Bridge

sheepfold ×

Strutta Wood

a 'surprise' view (less well-known than the one in Ashness Wood)

KESWICK 2½

Ashness Bridge

Waterfalls in Ashness Gill

ASCENT FROM WATENDLATH
1200 feet of ascent : 2 miles

HIGH SEAT

BLEABERRY FELL ←

→ Pouterhow Pike
conspicuous from below, but merely a steepening of the ground, not to be mistaken for the top!

1900

heather 1800

1700

sheepfold

heather

peat·hags   peat·hags

Fine cairn, good views

fort

a remarkable mound of stones, becoming overgrown with heather. Is this a tumulus?

HIGH TOVE

stile?

There is no firm footing for the traditional stone walls on the spongy upper slopes — hence the use of fences

1600

1500

gate

1300

Reecastle Crag
(The British Hill Fort here is a disappointment, there being no apparent evidences)

gate (to be climbed)

1400

Goat Crags

bracken

1200

The High Tove path leaves the junction as a grassy groove

the deep ravine of Raise Gill

Unfortunately, this alternative route starts with a gate marked NO ROAD. Well-mannered walkers will ask permission at the farm.

private farm·track

1300

WYTHBURN

1200

1100

1000

This is the well-known zig-zag exit from Watendlath (Public footpaths to Armboth and Wythburn) It has many variations up to the wall·corner

KESWICK (road) 5

The Churn

900

Watendlath

new dam

looking north-east

tarn

The quickest and most usual route visits High Tove by the Armboth path and then follows the fence, but, once Watendlath is out of sight, the way is very dreary and squelchy underfoot. The alternative (left) is an attempt to link together the few features of interest on this flank of High Seat, at the same time avoiding much of the worst of the wet ground.

Watendlath from Goat Crags

ASCENT FROM DALE BOTTOM
1600 feet of ascent : 4 miles (6½ from Keswick)

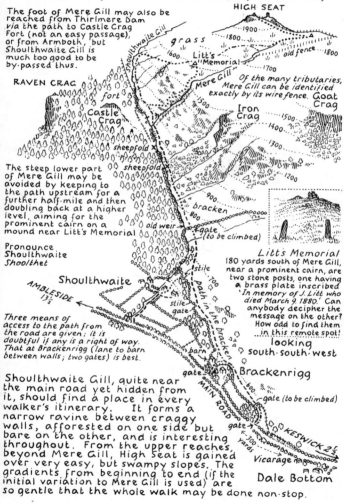

The foot of Mere Gill may also be reached from Thirlmere Dam via the path to Castle Crag Fort (not an easy passage), or from Armboth, but Shoulthwaite Gill is much too good to be by-passed thus.

HIGH SEAT

1900

1800

grass

Litt's Memorial

old fence 1800

1700

1600

RAVEN CRAG

Mere Gill

Of the many tributaries, Mere Gill can be identified exactly by its wire fence.

Goat Crag

Fort

Castle Crag

Iron Crag

1500

1400

1300

sheepfold X

1200

The steep lower part of Mere Gill may be avoided by keeping to the path upstream for a further half-mile and then doubling back at a higher level, aiming for the prominent cairn on a mound near Litt's Memorial

sheepfold X

900

800

bracken

old weir

gate (to be climbed)

Pronounce Shoulthwaite Shoolthet

Litt's Memorial
180 yards south of Mere Gill, near a prominent cairn, are two stone posts, one having a brass plate inscribed 'In memory of J. Litt who died March 9 1880.' Can anybody decipher the message on the other? How odd to find them in this remote spot!

Shoulthwaite

stile

700

AMBLESIDE 13½

stile
gate

path in the bracken

looking south-south-west

Three means of access to the path from the road are given; it is doubtful if any is a right of way. That at Brackenrigg (lane to barn between walls; two gates) is best.

barn

600

Brackenrigg

gate

MAIN ROAD

Shoulthwaite Gill, quite near the main road yet hidden from it, should find a place in every walker's itinerary. It forms a narrow ravine between craggy walls, afforested on one side but bare on the other, and is interesting throughout. From the upper reaches, beyond Mere Gill, High Seat is gained over very easy, but swampy slopes. The gradients from beginning to end (if the initial variation to Mere Gill is used) are so gentle that the whole walk may be done non-stop.

gate (to be climbed)

gate

KESWICK 2¼

500

yards

Vicarage

Dale Bottom

ASCENT FROM ARMBOTH, THIRLMERE
1450 feet of ascent : 2 miles

An obvious route of ascent leaves the west Thirlmere road at Armboth, where a signposted footpath to Watendlath may be used as far as the big cairn on High Tove summit and the fence then followed to the right. There is no point in doing this in clear weather, however, for it is much shorter and at least quite as easy to make a direct course to High Seat from the upper plantation wall (half-right), and the chances are that drier walking will be found by so doing.

THE SUMMIT

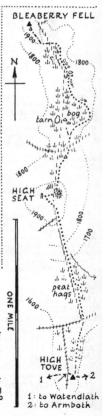

BLEABERRY FELL

The summit is a welcome dry oasis, with a few rocks to relieve the monotony of the surrounding swamps. An Ordnance Survey column marks the highest point, although there can be a difference of inches only between this and a prominent rock knoll called Man. The usually accepted height is 1995', but the 6" O.S. map shows a benchmark of 1996'. Adding to this the height of the column, it seems just possible that the triangulation plate might touch an altitude of 2000'.

DESCENTS: Routes of ascent may be reversed, the fences being a help in mist. Remember that there are crags on both flanks below 1500'. The Ashness Gill route needs care : get on the west bank

RIDGE ROUTES

To BLEABERRY FELL, 1932': 1¼ miles : N
Many small depressions : 150 feet of ascent

This is a walk to wish on one's worst enemy, especially after rain. There are many patches of swampy ground, necessitating wide detours.

To HIGH TOVE, 1665': 1 mile : S
Depression at 1650' : 25 feet of ascent

This is not a pleasant walk, either. The hags of rich deep peat may be wonderful stuff for growing rhododendrons but seem singularly unattractive to walkers with soaking feet.

1 : to Watendlath
2 : to Armboth

THE VIEW

High Seat is a first-class viewpoint, with much of interest to see in all directions. The serrated skyline from south to north-west is remarkably good and will gain most attention.

Principal Fells

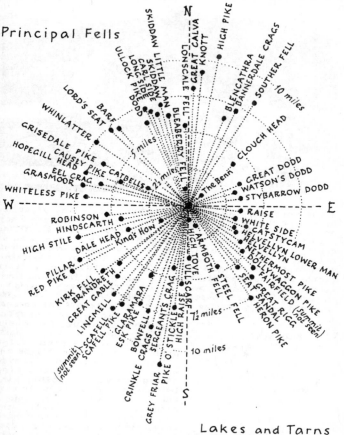

Lakes and Tarns
SE: Thirlmere (middle reach)
NW: Derwentwater
NW: Bassenthwaite Lake

High Tove

from Armboth Fell

It is hard to imagine that anybody feels any affection at all for High Tove, apart perhaps from the sheep whose natural heaf it is. This dark heathery mound, squatting on the ridge between Watendlath and Thirlmere, and so gently contoured that water cannot drain away from it, is everywhere shockingly wet — a condition persisting even in drought — and is without any redeeming feature except as a viewpoint. Yet it is climbed a thousand times every year, probably, and maybe more: the explanation is that High Tove is crossed by a public and fairly well used footpath that gives the shortest route across the central ridge. In fact, in this respect High Tove is unique, for where else is a summit used as a pass? This oddity arises because the depressions on either side are not only insignificant but even wetter than the way over the top.

A geographical curiosity is the twist in the indefinite north-east ridge, which, after ambling down easily towards, apparently, the obvious destination of Thirlmere unexpectedly changes character and rises again as a high rock rampart now heading due north in a heavy screen of trees to the abrupt, exciting top of Raven Crag.

HIGH SEAT ▲
Armboth ●
● ▲ HIGH TOVE
Watendlath
● Rosthwaite
Wythburn ●
▲ ULLSCARF

MILES
0   1   2   3   4

MAP

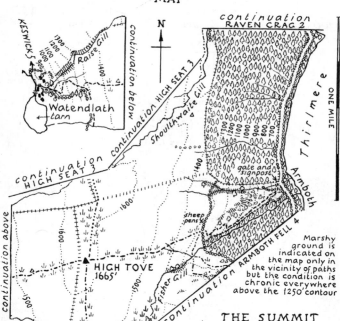

N

continuation RAVEN CRAG 2

KESWICK 5

Raise Gill

Watendlath tarn

continuation below

continuation HIGH SEAT 3

Shoulthwaite Gill

ONE MILE

Thirlmere

continuation
HIGH SEAT 2

continuation HIGH SEAT 3

continuation above

gate and signpost

Armboth

sheep pens

▲ HIGH TOVE 1665'

Fisher Gill

continuation ARMBOTH FELL 4

Marshy ground is indicated on the map only in the vicinity of paths but the condition is chronic everywhere above the 1250' contour

continuation
ARMBOTH FELL 3

THE SUMMIT

The public footpath between Watendlath and Armboth does not follow its original course nowadays (and, in fact, has not done so for decades). Confusion may arise because editions of maps still in current use do not show the new route. The change probably dates from the time of the Thirlmere plantings, for the path formerly *crossed* Fisher Gill, going down to the road on the south bank. It is not now possible to trace the original route. The diagram shows the new path in relation to the line of the original.

ONE MILE

old path   new path   A

W ×·×·×·×·× A ×·×·×·×·×·×·×·×·× Fisher Gill

new path   old path

The top has pretensions to beauty only when the heather is in bloom; for most of the year it is a dreary place, with no feature of interest. A big cairn offers a seat to travellers who wish to pour the water out of their boots. Nearby, in the old fence, there is a stile, now used by short-sighted hikers only.

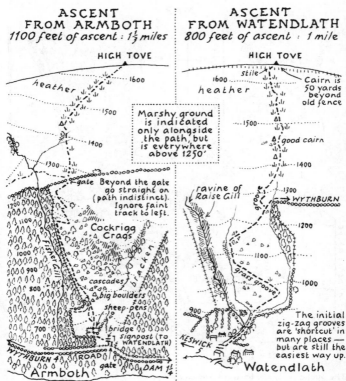

ASCENT FROM ARMBOTH
1100 feet of ascent : 1⅓ miles

HIGH TOVE

heather — 1600

— 1500

— 1400

— 1300

gate Beyond the gate go straight on (path indistinct). Ignore faint track to left.

Cockrigg Crags

Fisher Gill

bracken

cascades

big boulders

sheep-pens

bridge

signpost (to WATENDLATH)

WYTHBURN 4   ROAD   DAM 1¼
gate
Armboth

Thirlmere

looking west-south-west

Armboth still features prominently on maps and signposts, but the tired traveller should not expect to find refreshment or accommodation here. Nothing is left but the name.

Marshy ground is indicated only alongside the path, but is everywhere above 1250'

ASCENT FROM WATENDLATH
800 feet of ascent : 1 mile

HIGH TOVE

stile

heather — 1600   Cairn is 50 yards beyond old fence

— 1500

good cairn

— 1400

ravine of Raise Gill

groove — 1300

→ WYTHBURN

— 1200

grass groove

— 1100

— 1000

— 900

KESWICK 5 ←

The initial zig-zag grooves are 'shortcut' in many places — but are still the easiest way up.

Watendlath

At the wall-corner (at 1250') watch for a grass groove turning left : this is the path for High Tove (and on to Armboth), easily missed because the Wythburn path, which is stony, is the more distinct. The bifurcation is a few yards short of the wall-corner.

looking east

These two climbs have much in common —— and the greatest common factor is wetness on the ground, the last half-mile on both sides being saturated, both in rainy weather and in drought, and there is no escape from it. The two climbs are complementary, the path up one side and down the other being the public route between Armboth and Watendlath.

THE VIEW

The view is excellent westwards, but circumscribed to north and south.

Principal Fells

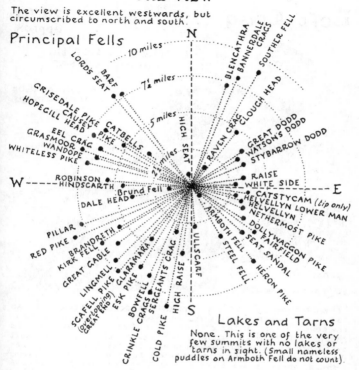

N

10 miles
7½ miles
5 miles
2½ miles

LORDS SEAT
BARF
GRISEDALE PIKE
CAUSEY PIKE
HOPEGILL HEAD
CATBELLS
EEL CRAG
GRASMOOR
WANDOPE
WHITELESS PIKE
ROBINSON
HINDSCARTH
DALE HEAD

HIGH SEAT

BLENCATHRA
BANNERDALE CRAGS
SOUTHER FELL
CLOUGH HEAD
RAVEN CRAG
GREAT DODD
WATSON'S DODD
STYBARROW DODD

W - - - - - Brund Fell - - - - - - - - - - E

RAISE
WHITE SIDE
CATSTYCAM (tip only)
HELVELLYN LOWER MAN
HELVELLYN
NETHERMOST PIKE
DOLLYWAGGON PIKE
FAIRFIELD
SEAT SANDAL
HERON PIKE

PILLAR
RED PIKE
BRANDRETH
KIRK FELL
GREAT GABLE
LINGMELL
SCAFELL PIKE
(overlapping)
GREAT END
ESK PIKE
BOWFELL
CRINKLE CRAGS
GLARAMARA
SERGEANTS CRAG
COLD PIKE
HIGH RAISE
ULLSCARF
STEEL FELL
ARMBOTH FELL

S

Lakes and Tarns

None. This is one of the very few summits with no lakes or tarns in sight. (Small nameless puddles on Armboth Fell do not count).

RIDGE ROUTES

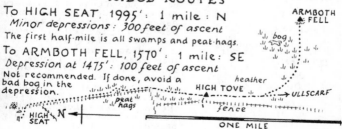

To HIGH SEAT, 1995': 1 mile : N
Minor depressions : 300 feet of ascent
The first half-mile is all swamps and peat-hags.

To ARMBOTH FELL, 1570': 1 mile : SE
Depression at 1475': 100 feet of ascent
Not recommended. If done, avoid a bad bog in the depression.

ARMBOTH FELL

bog

heather

HIGH TOVE
ULLSCARF

peat hags

fence

HIGH SEAT

N

ONE MILE

Loft Crag

2270'
approx.

the third of the
Langdale Pikes

not named on
Ordnance maps

from Pike o' Stickle

The Langdale Pikes are variously regarded as being from two to five in number. Thorn Crag and Pavey Ark, often included in the count, have not the distinctive outline of the others, and should perhaps more properly be omitted, but Loft Crag most certainly has the qualifying characteristics. It lies between Pike o' Stickle and Harrison Stickle but south of them, having a small, abrupt summit (often mistaken for Pike o' Stickle in views from the east) directly below which is the magnificent buttress of Gimmer Crag, most popular of all climbing-grounds.

Beyond Thorn Crag, a subsidiary summit, the deep-cut ravines of Dungeon Ghyll form the eastern boundary of the fell, but on the west side the line of demarcation is less exact, watercourses being submerged in rivers of scree. The short north slopes, after initial rocks, are soon lost in the wide depression of Harrison Combe.

Although it must rank after the two Stickles, Loft Crag is a worthy member of a fine trinity of peaks.

HIGH RAISE ▲

PIKE O'   ▲ ▲ HARRISON
STICKLE   STICKLE
LOFT CRAG
Old Hotel ●   ● New
              Hotel
Dungeon Ghyll

MILES

0   1   2   3

Gimmer Crag
South-east face

Loft Crag 3

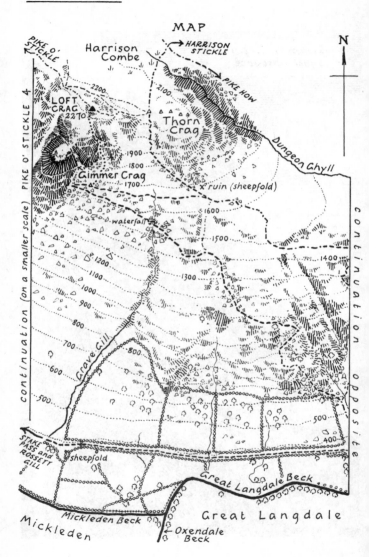

MAP

N

Harrison Combe

HARRISON STICKLE

PIKE O' STICKLE

PIKE HOW

LOFT CRAG 2270

Thorn Crag

Dungeon Ghyll

continuation opposite

PIKE O' STICKLE 4

Gimmer Crag

2200
2100
2000
1900
1800
1700
1600
1500
1400
1300
1200
1100
1000
900
800
700
600
500
400

x ruin (sheepfold)

waterfall

Grave Gill

continuation (on a smaller scale)

STAKE PASS and ROSSETT GILL

sheepfold

Great Langdale Beck

Great Langdale

Mickleden Beck

Oxendale Beck

Mickleden

MAP

NOTE that this map is on the specially large scale of SIX INCHES TO ONE MILE (as is the map of the fell adjoining, Harrison Stickle) in order to show essential detail more clearly.

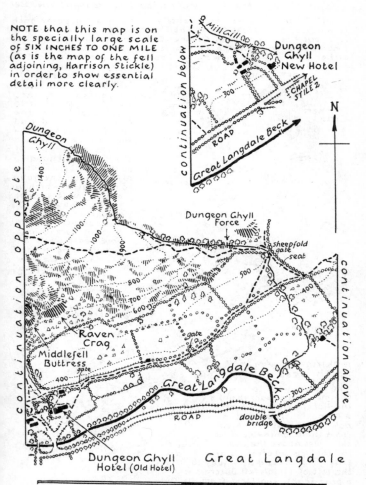

ASCENT FROM DUNGEON GHYLL
2,000 feet of ascent :
1¼ miles from the Old Hotel (direct): 1½ from the New Hotel

Loft Crag is reached most easily by using the popular path to Harrison Stickle as far as the Thorn Crag col, there turning left, but little is seen of Gimmer Crag on this route, and that fine rock is too grand a spectacle to miss. To see the crag, either turn off the path below Thorn Crag (cairn indicates traverse to it, left) or ascend direct from the Old Hotel. It will be palpable to the ordinary walker that progress has come to a full stop when the crag is reached, and the Thorn Crag path should then be joined for the remainder of the climb, although a possible alternative is afforded by the gully route shown, which is quite simple except for an awkward 10' chockstone pitch. Do not confuse this gully with the more obvious South-east Gully of Gimmer Crag: it is the next to the right (South-east Gully is a recognised rock-climb (graded easy). Active walkers will probably find it within their capacity, but others are advised to turn their backs on it).

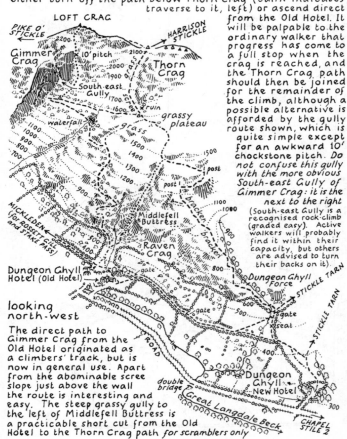

LOFT CRAG
PIKE O' STICKLE
HARRISON STICKLE
Gimmer Crag
10' pitch
Thorn Crag
South-east Gully
ruin
grassy plateau
waterfall
grass
post
post
MICKLEDEN (for ROSSETT GILL and STAKE PASS)
Middlefell Buttress
bracken
bracken
Raven Crag
Dungeon Ghyll Hotel (Old Hotel)
Dungeon Ghyll Force
STICKLE TARN
gate
seat
gate
STICKLE TARN
ROAD
double bridge
Dungeon Ghyll New Hotel
Great Langdale Beck
CHAPEL STILE 2

looking north-west

The direct path to Gimmer Crag from the Old Hotel originated as a climbers' track, but is now in general use. Apart from the abominable scree slope just above the wall the route is interesting and easy. The steep grassy gully to the left of Middlefell Buttress is a practicable short cut from the Old Hotel to the Thorn Crag path *for scramblers only*

THE SUMMIT

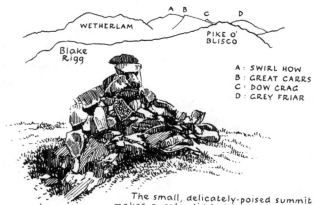

WETHERLAM

Blake Rigg

PIKE O' BLISCO

A: SWIRL HOW
B: GREAT CARRS
C: DOW CRAG
D: GREY FRIAR

The small, delicately-poised summit makes a splendid halting-place, both for a survey of the fells around the head of Langdale and for its own comfortable bilberry couches, whether fruit-bearing or not. This airy top is the natural end to every climb on Gimmer Crag directly below, but it is a commentary on modern rockclimbers here, as elsewhere, that few of them really complete the ascent by visiting the summit. Rockclimbing is losing its affinity with fellwalking and becoming a thing apart. For the fellwalker the ultimate objective must always be the highest cairn.

DESCENTS: A faint track traverses the short ridge, linking with a path that skirts the northern base of the summit and goes to the right to join the Thorn Crag col route to Dungeon Ghyll. In clear weather only, the route by the 10' chockstone-pitch may be used to see Gimmer Crag at close quarters before joining the usual paths to the valley.
(The TOP of Gimmer Crag may be visited by an easy traverse from just above the 10' pitch, as shown in the diagram)

1: to Pike o'Stickle
2: to Thorn Crag col
3: Gimmer Crag
4: Junipal Gully

view of north-west face of Gimmer Crag

100 YARDS

North-west gully (scree)

N

grass traverse

grassy top of Gimmer Crag

10' pitch

Southeast gully

path

THE VIEW

The view is not so extensive as that from either of the two adjacent Pikes, but, because Loft Crag thrusts further into Langdale than the others, the prospect of that valley and the lakes around its foot is even better. Bowfell rises majestically from the depths of Mickleden.

Principal Fells

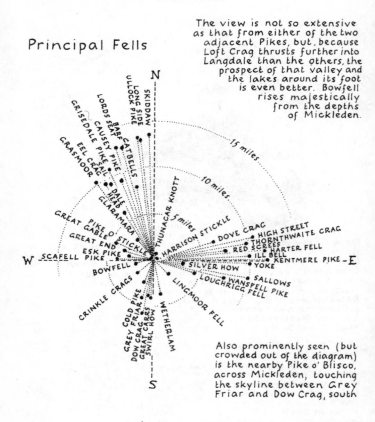

Also prominently seen (but crowded out of the diagram) is the nearby Pike o' Blisco, across Mickleden, touching the skyline between Grey Friar and Dow Crag, south

Lakes and Tarns

E : Tarns by Lang How (Silver How)
ESE : Loughrigg Tarn
ESE : Elterwater
SE : Windermere
SE : Lingmoor Tarn
SE : Esthwaite Water
SSE : Blea Tarn
NNW : Tarn at Leaves (Rosthwaite Fell)

RIDGE ROUTES

To HARRISON STICKLE, 2403':
½ mile : E, then N and E
Depression at 2070'
340 feet of ascent
Care is needed in getting off the
east end of Loft Crag: at the first
depression use a little scree-run
on the left. At Thorn Crag *col* join
the usual path from Langdale.

To PIKE O' STICKLE, 2323':
⅓ mile : NW
Two depressions at 2200'
170 feet of ascent
An interesting path follows the
ridge. The final scramble is
steep and rocky, and permits
of minor variations

These are large-scale maps

HALF A MILE

This is the 10-foot
chockstone pitch
mentioned in the
diagram of ascent
.......(page 5).......

*Pike o' Stickle
from Loft Crag*

Loughrigg Fell

1101'

more often referred to
simply as 'Loughrigg'
(pronounced Luffrigg)

SILVER ▲ HOW
• Grasmere
▲
LOUGHRIGG FELL • Rydal
• Ambleside
• Clappersgate
• Skelwith Bridge

MILES
0 1 2 3 4

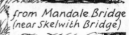

*from Mandale Bridge
(near Skelwith Bridge)*

NATURAL FEATURES

Of the lesser heights of Lakeland, Loughrigg Fell is pre-eminent. It has no pretensions to mountain form, being a sprawling, ill-shaped wedge of rough country rising between the park-like valleys of Brathay and Rothay, and having a bulk out of all proportion to its modest altitude; but no ascent is more repaying for the small labour involved in visiting its many cairns, for Loughrigg has delightful grassy paths, a series of pleasant surprises along the traverse of the summits, several charming vistas and magnificent views, fine contrasts of velvety turf, rich bracken and grey rock, a string of little tarns like pearls in a necklace, and a wealth of stately trees on the flanks. It is especially well endowed with lakes, with four sheets of water, all lovely, touching its lower slopes, and in addition it nurses a large tarn to which it gives its name — and this is a distinction not attained by any other fell. It has also more paths to the square mile than any other fell, great or small, and amongst them is one that far exceeds in popularity any other in the district, one that all visitors know: Loughrigg Terrace. Short crags on every flank offer excellent sport for the rock-scrambler. Woodlands surround the base of the fell and creep up the slopes; higher, juniper holly and yew straggle the fellside. Loughrigg has yet another attraction in the form of a tremendous cave, big enough to contain the entire population of Ambleside, which, although manmade and now disused, is still a remarkable place. In brief, this fell has a wealth of interests and delights, and for many people who now find pleasure in walking over the greater mountains it served as an introduction and an inspiration. Everybody likes Loughrigg.

Topographically, Loughrigg Fell is the corner-stone of the high mass of land lying south-west of the Rothay valley system, with High Raise as the loftiest point, but is almost isolated, the connecting link being a low and indefinite ridge crossed by the Red Bank road between Grasmere and Langdale. The fell, two miles long, has subsidiary summits overlooking each of the surrounding lakes.

MAP

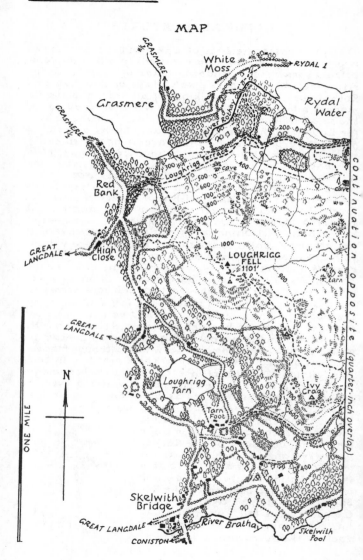

MAP

Note that the scale of this map is larger than that commonly used in this book

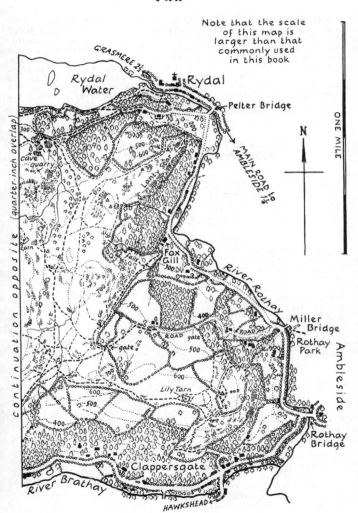

ASCENTS

When fellwalking, it is better to arrive than to travel hopefully and this is justification for the inclusion here of six pages of directions for reaching the summit of Loughrigg Fell, because, although of insignificant altitude, the fell has an extensive and confusing top, the ultimate objective remains hidden on the approach, and the maze of paths needs careful unravelling — besides, failure would be *too* humiliating! On a first visit it is not only not easy to locate the highest point amongst the score of likely-looking protuberances several of which carry likely-looking cairns, it is actually difficult not to go astray, and, in mist, positively easy to do so.

ASCENT FROM GRASMERE
920 feet of ascent : 2¼ miles

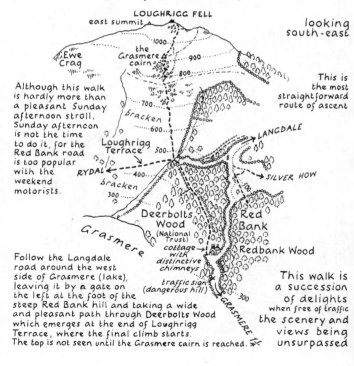

LOUGHRIGG FELL
east summit

looking south-east

Ewe Crag

the Grasmere cairn

1000

900

800

This is the most straightforward route of ascent

Although this walk is hardly more than a pleasant Sunday afternoon stroll, Sunday afternoon is not the time to do it, for the Red Bank road is too popular with the weekend motorists.

700

bracken

600

LANGDALE

Loughrigg Terrace   500

RYDAL   400

bracken

300

SILVER HOW

Deerbolts Wood (National Trust)

Red Bank

Grasmere

cottage with distinctive chimneys

traffic sign (dangerous hill)

Redbank Wood

300

GRASMERE

Follow the Langdale road around the west side of Grasmere (lake), leaving it by a gate on the left at the foot of the steep Red Bank hill and taking a wide and pleasant path through Deerbolts Wood which emerges at the end of Loughrigg Terrace, where the final climb starts.
The top is not seen until the Grasmere cairn is reached.

This walk is a succession of delights when free of traffic the scenery and views being unsurpassed

ASCENT FROM AMBLESIDE
1050 feet of ascent : 2½ miles

LOUGHRIGG FELL

south summit • east summit

viewpoint for Loughrigg Farm

good viewpoint for Windermere

Ivy Crag

1000

tarns

900

bracken

800

700

tarns

bracken

600

SKELWITH BRIDGE — tarn — — A — — — A — A — RYDAL

Troughton Gill

A stands for Amphitheatre
— a shallow depression, once
used as a rifle range and
now a meeting-place of many paths

gate

600

former golf course
(club disbanded 1956
— lack of support)

former clubhouse
(now private residence)

500

Juniper

gate

private grounds

rhododendron thickets; path along fence

signpost

TODD CRAG

400

stile

300

Browhead Farm

private grounds

Fox Gill

RYDAL

300

Loughrigg Brow

200

Fox How

unusual wall of stone slabs

private grounds

River Rothay

looking west

ROTHAY BRIDGE ½

Miller Bridge

Rothay Park

useful little building

school

St. Mary's Church

Ambleside

A beautiful walk, to be done
leisurely. The usual route
is by way of Browhead Farm
but the path from Fox Gill
has, initially, an intimate
charm all its own, although
inferior in views.

ASCENT FROM RYDAL
1000 feet of ascent : 2½ miles

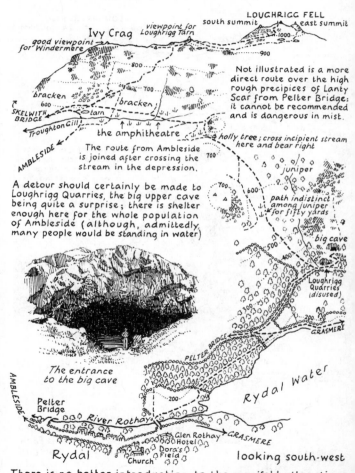

LOUGHRIGG FELL
south summit — east summit

viewpoint for
Loughrigg Tarn

Ivy Crag

good viewpoint
for Windermere

1000

900

800

700

600

bracken

bracken

SKELWITH
BRIDGE

tarn

Troughton Gill

AMBLESIDE

the amphitheatre

The route from Ambleside
is joined after crossing the
stream in the depression.

Not illustrated is a more
direct route over the high
rough precipices of Lanty
Scar from Pelter Bridge:
it cannot be recommended
and is dangerous in mist.

a holly tree; cross incipient stream
here and bear right

700

juniper

700

600

path indistinct
among juniper
for fifty yards

500

400

big cave

A detour should certainly be made to
Loughrigg Quarries, the big upper cave
being quite a surprise; there is shelter
enough here for the whole population
of Ambleside (although, admittedly,
many people would be standing in water)

300

200

Loughrigg
Quarries
(disused)

GRASMERE

PELTER BRIDGE

200

*The entrance
to the big cave*

AMBLESIDE

Pelter
Bridge

River Rothay

200

Rydal Water

GRASMERE

Glen Rothay
Hotel

Rydal

Church

Dora's
Field

looking south-west

There is no better introduction to the manifold attractions
of Loughrigg Fell than this easy and delightful approach.

ASCENT FROM WHITE MOSS
925 feet of ascent : 1½ miles

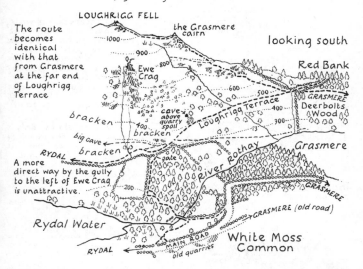

LOUGHRIGG FELL

the Grasmere cairn

looking south

The route becomes identical with that from Grasmere at the far end of Loughrigg Terrace

Red Bank

Ewe Crag

GRASMERE

Deerbolts Wood

Loughrigg Terrace

bracken

cave above quarry spoil

bracken

big cave

bracken

RYDAL

Grasmere

A more direct way by the gully to the left of Ewe Crag is unattractive.

gate

River Rothay

GRASMERE

Rydal Water

RYDAL

GRASMERE (old road)

MAIN ROAD

old quarries

White Moss Common

This might be described as 'the motorist's route', not because it is practicable for cars (!) but because White Moss Common is a popular parking place and the most convenient point on the road for starting the climb.

Grasmere
from Loughrigg Terrace

ASCENT FROM CLAPPERSGATE
1050 feet of ascent : 2½ miles

LOUGHRIGG FELL
south summit   east summit

Ivy Crag

1000
tarn
900

tarns

800

700   → RYDAL

SKELWITH
BRIDGE
600   tarn   → AMBLESIDE

700

*looking
north-west*

bracken

500

this is the
official
Todd Crag
(Ordnance Survey 2½" map)

Lily Tarn

Todd Crag

This interesting walk, combined with a descent from the summit by the Grasmere path enables a full-length traverse of the fell to be made : an easy and enjoyable excursion. Detours should be made to Todd Crag and Ivy Crag, both excellent viewpoints.

There is a tiny island, only a few feet in extent, in the middle of Lily Tarn. Some quiet humorist has erected a cairn on it.

tarn

600

× site of
old building

striking view of
Windermere from
Todd Crag

500

bracken

pivvle

400

300   300

gate

Here are the
gardens of
White Craggs,
open to the public

200   kiosk

Clappersgate

SKELWITH BRIDGE

River Brathay   Brathay
Bridge

HAWKSHEAD

*The
summit of
Todd Crag, showing the 10-foot crack*

Todd Crag dominates the initial part of the climb, and its summit, a small platform of naked rock, is worth a visit. It can be reached easily by a short scramble, but persons more agile than the author may prefer to attain it in more dramatic fashion by struggling up a 10 foot crack on the east side.

Similar rocky heights nearby are also interesting.

Leave Clappersgate by the lane directly opposite the road junction

ASCENT FROM SKELWITH BRIDGE
1000 feet of ascent: 1¾ miles

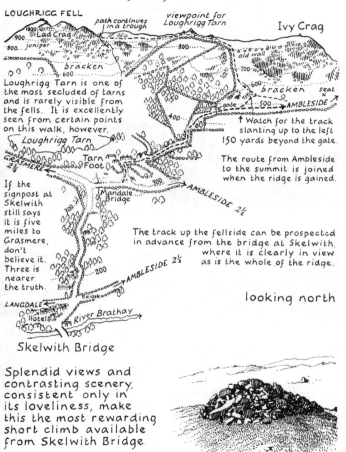

LOUGHRIGG FELL

path continues in a trough

viewpoint for Loughrigg Tarn

Ivy Crag

1000 — Lad Crag — 900 — juniper — 800 — bracken — 600 — 800 — 700 — old wall — 600 — bracken — seat — 500 — AMBLESIDE — 400 — gate

Loughrigg Tarn is one of the most secluded of tarns and is rarely visible from the fells. It is excellently seen from certain points on this walk, however.

Loughrigg Tarn

GRASMERE 2¾

Tarn Foot

Mandale Bridge — 300 — AMBLESIDE 2½

200

AMBLESIDE 2½

If the signpost at Skelwith still says it is five miles to Grasmere, don't believe it. Three is nearer the truth.

LANGDALE Hotels ½

kiosk

River Brathay

↑ Watch for the track slanting up to the left 150 yards beyond the gate.

The route from Ambleside to the summit is joined when the ridge is gained.

The track up the fellside can be prospected in advance from the bridge at Skelwith, where it is clearly in view as is the whole of the ridge.

looking north

Skelwith Bridge

Splendid views and contrasting scenery, consistent only in its loveliness, make this the most rewarding short climb available from Skelwith Bridge.

The cairn on Ivy Crag
a good viewpoint for Windermere and Langdale,
reached by a simple detour along the ridge.

THE SUMMIT

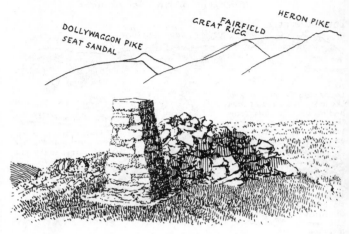

Three eminences rise close together above the undulating top of the fell, and the middle one, slightly higher than the others, bears the main cairn and an Ordnance Survey triangulation column that the surveyors who built it, after building so many, must have voted the most beautifully situated of all. The small area of the principal summit is carpeted with a velvety turf in which have been carved the initials of many visitors. There are several tarns, little more than dewponds, in the green hollows around. Bracken encroaches in patches on the higher parts of the fell and, especially in winter, makes the summit a colourful place.

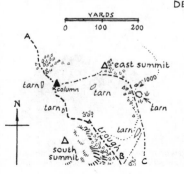

DESCENTS : There are hundreds of rocky tors and low crags scattered about the fell top and descents are most easily made by using the paths, of which there is also a great abundance. The quickest way down (and the best in mist) is by the Grasmere route to Loughrigg Terrace.

A : to Grasmere and Loughrigg Terrace
B : to Ambleside, Clappersgate Rydal and Skelwith Bridge
C : an alternative to B (joins it in a further quarter-mile)

RIDGE ROUTE

To SILVER HOW, 1292': 2½ miles
NW, then W, WNW and N
Several depressions; main one 475'
950 feet of ascent
A sharp descent is followed by
a beautiful and easy walk

SILVER HOW!

BLEA RIGG

1200 1000

GRASMERE

LANGDALE

Spedding Crag

900 800

WALTHWAITE

Dow Bank

At this col, climb half-right between low crags (no path)

Viewpoint for Rydal and ruin Grasmere

GRASMERE (road)

HALF A MILE

N

Red Bank

Loughrigg Terrace

500 600 700

800 900

GRASMERE

GRASMERE

ELTERWATER line of telegraph poles

700 600

ELTERWATER (road)

AMBLESIDE (road)

1000

LOUGHRIGG FELL

Make the little detour to the two cairns on Spedding Crag, where there is a striking birds-eye view of Chapel Stile and Walthwaite

Dow Bank is the most prominent rise on the ridge, the climb to it being steep

This pleasant stroll is full of interest and variety: it has lake and woodland scenes, rocky outcrops, a few yards of macadam(!) and its gentle undulations are crossed by favourite paths from Grasmere to Langdale. The views are delightful on all sides. In bad weather do not proceed beyond the final col unless the ground is well known; paths on Silver How are a source of trouble in mist.

Loughrigg Tarn

THE VIEW

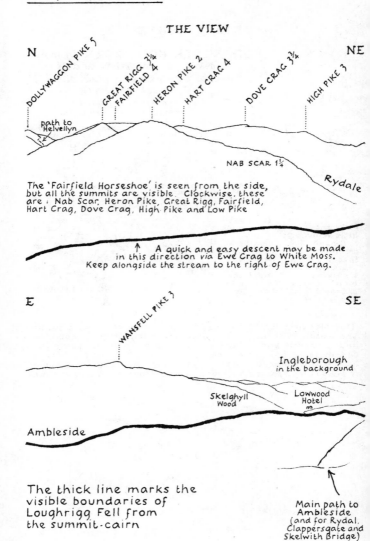

N   NE

DOLLYWAGGON PIKE 5 — GREAT RIGG 2¾ — FAIRFIELD 4 — HERON PIKE 2 — HART CRAG 4 — DOVE CRAG 3¾ — HIGH PIKE 3

path to Helvellyn

NAB SCAR 1¼

Rydale

The 'Fairfield Horseshoe' is seen from the side, but all the summits are visible. Clockwise, these are : Nab Scar, Heron Pike, Great Rigg, Fairfield, Hart Crag, Dove Crag, High Pike and Low Pike

A quick and easy descent may be made in this direction via Ewe Crag to White Moss. Keep alongside the stream to the right of Ewe Crag.

E   SE

WANSFELL PIKE 3

Ingleborough in the background

Skelghyll Wood

Lowwood Hotel

Ambleside

The thick line marks the visible boundaries of Loughrigg Fell from the summit-cairn

Main path to Ambleside (and for Rydal, Clappersgate and Skelwith Bridge)

THE VIEW

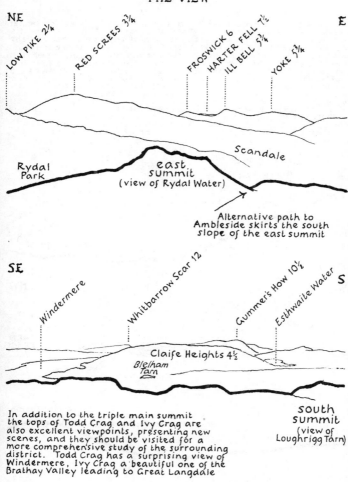

NE

LOW PIKE 2¼ — RED SCREES 3¾ — FROSWICK 6 — HARTER FELL 7½ — ILL BELL 5¾ — YOKE 5¾

E

Scandale

Rydal Park

east summit
(view of Rydal Water)

Alternative path to Ambleside skirts the south slope of the east summit

SE

Windermere — Whitbarrow Scar 12 — Gummer's How 10½ — Esthwaite Water

S

Claife Heights 4½

Blelham Tarn

south summit
(view of Loughrigg Tarn)

In addition to the triple main summit the tops of Todd Crag and Ivy Crag are also excellent viewpoints, presenting new scenes, and they should be visited for a more comprehensive study of the surrounding district. Todd Crag has a surprising view of Windermere, Ivy Crag a beautiful one of the Brathay Valley leading to Great Langdale

The figures following the names of fells indicate distances in miles

THE VIEW

Anybody spending a first holiday in Ambleside cannot do better than make an early visit to the top of Loughrigg Fell.   From this elevation he will get an excellent idea of the topography of the neighbourhood, all the fells and valleys within easy reach being attractively displayed.   He will see around him a land very rich in promise — and find it even richer in fulfilment. The following fellwalks suggest themselves for a week's stay: 1 - THE FAIRFIELD HORSESHOE;   2 - THE CONISTON FELLS (ridgewalk, Wetherlam to Old Man) 3 - BOWFELL and CRINKLE CRAGS;   4 - HARRISON STICKLE, SERGEANT MAN and the SILVER HOW ridge;   5 - THE EASEDALE FELLS (circuit of Far Easedale) 6 - DOLLYWAGGON PIKE and HELVELLYN.   Of course the separate ascents of RED SCREES and WANSFELL PIKE cannot possibly be omitted — if time is short, these two climbs should be done before breakfast (best part of the day for fellwalking) on the day of departure. A better plan, however, is to stay on for another week, for the suggested itinerary by no means exhausts the area's attractions.

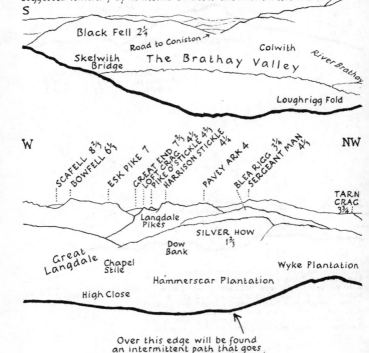

Over this edge will be found
an intermittent path that goes
down (between walls) to the road
near the grounds of High Close.

THE VIEW

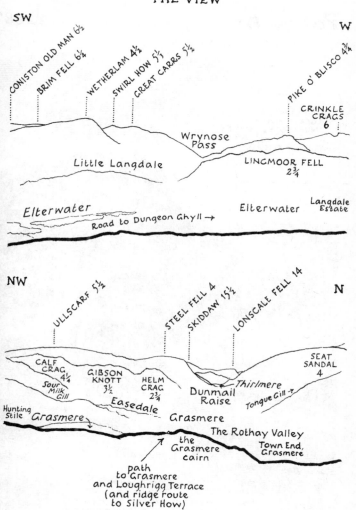

SW

W

CONISTON OLD MAN 6½
BRIM FELL 6¼
WETHERLAM 4½
SWIRL HOW 5⅓
GREAT CARRS 5½
PIKE O' BLISCO 4¾
CRINKLE CRAGS 6

Wrynose Pass

Little Langdale

LINGMOOR FELL 2¾

Elterwater

Road to Dungeon Ghyll →

Elterwater

Langdale Estate

NW

N

ULLSCARF 5½
STEEL FELL 4
SKIDDAW 13½
LONSCALE FELL 14

CALF CRAG 4¼
GIBSON KNOTT 3½
HELM CRAG 2¾
SEAT SANDAL 4

Sour Milk Gill

Easedale

Dunmail Raise

Thirlmere

Tongue Gill →

Hunting Stile

Grasmere

Grasmere

the Grasmere cairn

The Rothay Valley

Town End, Grasmere

path to Grasmere and Loughrigg Terrace (and ridge route to Silver How)

Pavey Ark

2288'

HIGH RAISE ▲
SERGEANT MAN ▲
THUNACAR ▲▲ PAVEY
KNOTT ARK

HARRISON STICKLE
●
Dungeon Ghyll

0　1　2　3
MILES

from the western slopes of Blea Rigg

NATURAL FEATURES

Pavey Ark is Langdale's biggest cliff. In an area where crags and precipices abound, here is the giant of them all, and, scenically, it is the best. The view of the Ark across the waters of Stickle Tarn, at its foot, is superior to all others of this type in Lakeland, having an advantage over the principal rival team of Dow Crag—Goats Water in that the scene, being invariably reached by the steep climb from Dungeon Ghyll, bursts upon the eye with dramatic effect. The crag itself has been superseded in the esteem of climbers by Gimmer Crag and other rock-faces nearer the valley, but is still a great favourite, and Stickle Tarn has many visitors.

It is usual to think of Pavey Ark as a crag, not as a fell. In a strict geographical sense the crag is the eastern boundary of Thunacar Knott, to which the ground above the crag gradually rises. But the Ark has its own proud little summit, an exhilarating place of grey rock, small tarns and soft vegetation that, in interest and charm, quite puts to shame the dreary top of the main fell. At the risk of offending Thunacar Knott, Pavey Ark must have a chapter to itself. The area to be covered is no more than a square half-mile but it is full of good things.

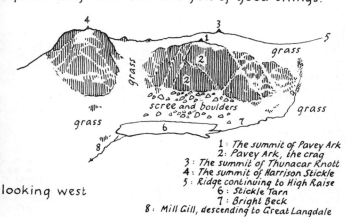

looking west

1 : The summit of Pavey Ark
2 : Pavey Ark, the crag
3 : The summit of Thunacar Knott
4 : The summit of Harrison Stickle
5 : Ridge continuing to High Raise
6 : Stickle Tarn
7 : Bright Beck
8 : Mill Gill, descending to Great Langdale

MAP

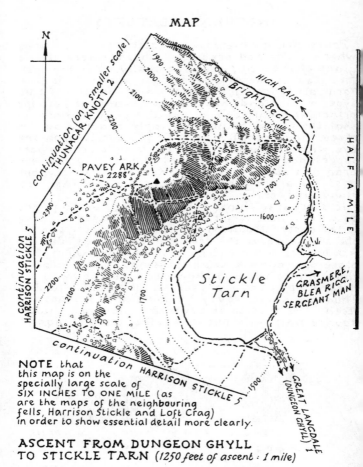

NOTE that
this map is on the
specially large scale of
SIX INCHES TO ONE MILE (as
are the maps of the neighbouring
fells, Harrison Stickle and Loft Crag)
in order to show essential detail more clearly.

ASCENT FROM DUNGEON GHYLL
TO STICKLE TARN (1250 feet of ascent : 1 mile)

Pavey Ark overlooks Great Langdale
and the natural (and only direct) route of ascent is
from that valley. Stickle Tarn is a place of popular
resort, and on most summer days it is only necessary
to follow the crowds, but if a diagram and details are
required, refer to Harrison Stickle 10. From Stickle Tarn
onwards, consult the following pages in this chapter.

ASCENTS FROM STICKLE TARN

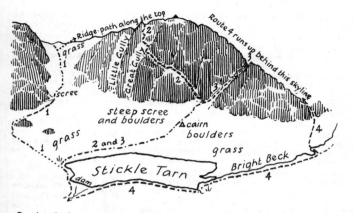

Pedestrian routes only are indicated, but the inclusion of Jack's Rake as such is subject to the qualification that the pedestrian must be agile and have flexible limbs and joints.

1 : An easy but tedious route that avoids the crag altogether, and is therefore something of a cheat.   This is the usual path to Harrison Stickle from the tarn, but it may be used for Pavey Ark by working to the right when the skyline is reached and so joining the good ridge-path that leads to the summit-cairn.

2 : Jack's Rake, about which a wealth of gruesome detail is to be found on the next two pages. This is a rock-climb rather than a walk. The rock scenery is very impressive.

3 : Easy Gully, an interesting route, without difficulty except at one point where a long stride upwards may prove too much for short-legged individuals. The gully runs into the North Rake at two-thirds the height of the latter. There are intimate views of the East Buttress. A diagram appears on page 7.

4 : North Rake, a surprising and remarkable grassy breach in the crags, cleaving them from top to bottom on their north side, and affording a simple route of ascent. It is not visible from Stickle Tarn and its presence is not suspected. (It is well seen from high on the slopes of Blea Rigg opposite). This route is recommended to persons who do not like handling rocks and to the short-legged individuals who have suffered defeat in Easy Gully, but is too remote from the main face of the Ark to yield good views. A fair path is developing along the Rake.
Officially, this route has no name, but it deserves one. North Rake seems as appropriate as any. There is a diagram on page 7.

ASCENT via JACK'S RAKE

Jack's Rake is classified as a ROCK CLIMB. Its grading is *easy* — it is the easiest of the recognised climbs in the Langdale area.

Nonetheless, as a WALK it is both *difficult* and *awkward*: in fact, for much of the way the body is propelled forwards by a series of convulsions unrelated to normal walking, the knees and elbows contributing as much to progress as hands and feet. Walkers who can still put their toes in their mouths and bring their knees up to their chins may embark upon the ascent confidently; others, unable to perform these tests, will find the route arduous.

The most awkward scrambling occurs in the initial section, to the third ashtree. Once fairly started, it is easier to go on than to retreat. The upper parts are enjoyable. The humble walker is rarely afforded such an opportunity to enter the realm of the climber, and the rock scenery is magnificent throughout.

Although the Rake climbs high across the face of a fearful precipice, there is curiously little sense of exposure, for a comforting parapet of rock accompanies all the steeper parts of the ascent. The character of the climbing changes when Great Gully is reached.

Care should be taken to avoid falling down the precipice or sending stones over the edge. Falling bodies, human or mineral, may constitute a danger to unseen climbers on the rocks or the scree below, or to grazing sheep.

looking back to the platform below Gwynnes Chimney, from the easy terrace

looking up the Rake to the groove leading to Great Gully, from the easy terrace

It should be noted that the grooves of the Rake form a natural drainage channel

(Significantly, both sketches are from the easy terrace, the only section where the author's mind was not fully occupied with a primitive desire for survival)

for water from the rocks above, and will therefore be wet after rain, thus adding further to the discomforts of the journey. Mist or high winds need not deter an ascent, but snow or ice put the Rake out of bounds decisively.

Jack's Rake is just about the limit that the ordinary common garden or fell walker reasonably may be expected to attempt.

continued

ASCENT via JACK'S RAKE

continued

This diagram will make more sense if it is read from the bottom upwards

From the top exit of Jack's Rake, the summit cairn is 100 yards to the right. Elated by their achievement, most pedestrians tackle the fine rocks on the right and so gain the cairn without crossing the summit-wall

top of Great Gully

summit-wall

pinnacle

perched boulder

Little Gully

Great Gully

15 YARDS: easy walk from depression to summit-wall

40 YARDS: Horizontal path to the left leads from Great Gully to an open area of big rock steps, where there is a choice of routes. Easy climbing. Aim for the depression to the *right* of the pinnacle

15 YARDS: path turns right and ascends gully
Great Gully is reached. Pinnacle comes into view

25 YARDS: easier rock groove becoming a channel

steep rock wall

Gwynne's Chimney

Several rock-climbs from the base of the crag finish up the steep grass below Gwynne's Chimney

15 YARDS: easy terrace
10 YARDS: steep groove (awkward start)

platform (foot of Gwynne's Chimney)

8 YARDS: slight descent (above steep grass slope – care!)

steep grass

steep rock wall

25 YARDS: easier climbing on more open slope (*the steepest part of the precipice is directly below*)

third ashtree

→ path turns slightly right

steep rock wall

40 YARDS: steep rock groove (*the worst section*)

Rake End Chimney

second ashtree

East Buttress

5 YARDS: easy platform (foot of Rake End Chimney) → *first ashtree*
15 YARDS: steep rock groove
20 YARDS: easy path on grass

Start from the base of the East Buttress (foot of Easy Gully)

All distances are approximate

scree

boulder slope

big cairn, with built-in tablet.

JWS 1900

STICKLE TARN OUTLET

> Total length of Rake: 225 yards.
> 400 feet of ascent at average angle of 30°
> (but 50° in steepest sections)

ASCENTS via EASY GULLY and NORTH RAKE

View from top of Easy Gully

The Coniston Fells
1: Wetherlam
2: Coniston Old Man
3: Swirl How
4: Great Carrs

Stickle Tarn

↖ Path continues to summit-cairn over grassy top of fell

Easy Gully is mainly a steep walk on grass and sliding scree, but near the top the gully is completely blocked by huge boulders (good shelter here), and for 50 feet the route lies over them, with one awkward obstacle

boulders

NORTH RAKE

looking west

East Buttress

Jack's Rake

Easy Gully levels out at the top and joins the North Rake by a grass path

EASY GULLY

big cairn

To locate North Rake from below, follow the course of the main feeder of Stickle Tarn (Bright Beck) for 300 yards by an improving path on the east bank. Here the path crosses the beck and slants up rightwards to the foot of the Rake

HIGH RAISE

Stickle Tarn

Bright Beck

If ascending by North Rake make the short detour to the top of Easy Gully for the view

STICKLE TARN OUTLET

→ SERGEANT MAN and BLEA RIGG

The North Rake

← Easy Gully joins here

North Rake starts with a little scree gully, then, after a short turn to the left, is a perfectly straight grassy uphill trudge, confined between crags. At the top, turn left to reach the cairn in 200 yards, crossing a broken wall midway. This is a surprisingly easy way to the summit, without difficulties of any sort. It deserves to be far better known. Try it sometime!

THE SUMMIT

The environs of the summit-cairn are delectable. Slabs and walls of beautiful grey rock, of rough texture not unlike the gabbro of Skye, rise from pleasant bilberry terraces, and some exploration is permissible here, with care, above the steepening precipices.

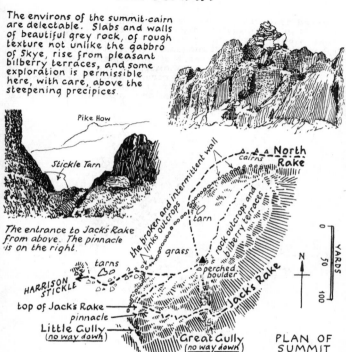

Pike How

Stickle Tarn

The entrance to Jack's Rake from above. The pinnacle is on the right.

PLAN OF SUMMIT

North Rake

cairns

the broken and intermittent wall links outcrops

tarn

grass

rock outcrops and bilberry terraces

HARRISON STICKLE

tarns

perched boulder

Jack's Rake

top of Jack's Rake
pinnacle
Little Gully (no way down)

Great Gully (no way down)

N

0
50
100

YARDS

DESCENTS (TO STICKLE TARN): The North Rake is the best for descent and is virtually fool-proof, even in mist. (Easy Gully, leading from it, is NOT a time-saver). If, alternatively, the Harrison Stickle–Stickle Tarn path is used, it should be joined high up over easy ground. Jack's Rake should be used as a way down only by walkers who have previously (and recently) ascended by this route and are aware of the difficulties. The place where the Rake leaves the top cannot be seen from the summit-cairn. It MUST be identified EXACTLY (see plan and illustration above). Keep strictly to the path (in places no more than nail-scratches on rocks) and assume that deviations will end fatally.

- -

The omission of RIDGE ROUTES from this chapter is not due to an oversight, but to the fact that Pavey Ark is not a point on a ridge. (See Thunacar Knott 4).

THE VIEW

Seated comfortably with his back against the cairn, one leg pointing to Loughrigg Fell and the other to Lingmoor Fell, the walker finds reward for his toil, for between his feet is a gem of a view: that of Great Langdale's graceful curves continued by the long sylvan upper reach of Windermere, a view greatly enhanced by the steep plunge of the ground immediately beyond his boots. In other directions the view is marred by a dull middle distance.

Principal Fells

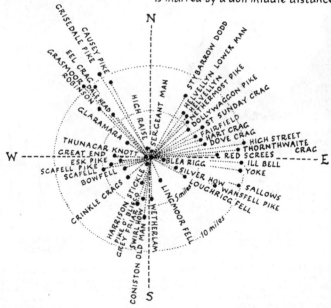

Lakes and Tarns

ESE: *Rydal Water*
SE: *Windermere (two sections)*
SE: *Loughrigg Tarn*
SE: *Elterwater*
SE: *Wise Een Tarn*
SE: *Esthwaite Water*
SSE: *Lingmoor Tarn*
SSE: *Stickle Tarn*
S: *Blea Tarn*

Pavey Ark

Pike o' Stickle

2323'

the second of the
Langdale Pikes

Pike OF Stickle,
to be correct

from Gimmer Crag

HIGH RAISE ▲

PIKE O'
STICKLE ▲ ▲ HARRISON
STICKLE

LOFT CRAG ▲
Old Hotel ● ● New
Hotel

Dungeon Ghyll

MILES

0   1   2   3

NATURAL FEATURES

Simple lines are often the most effective, and the smoothly-soaring pyramid of Pike o' Stickle, rising to a tapering thimble of rock without interruption or halt between valley and summit, is an imposing and impressive feature that contributes much to the grandeur of the head of Great Langdale. The unbroken sweep of Stickle Breast above Mickleden is one of the most continuously steep slopes in the district, rising nearly 2,000 feet over a lateral distance of half a mile. Dry scree gullies sever the craggy upper storey from the neighbouring fellsides, but a lofty ridge connects it with the castellated skyline overlooking Dungeon Ghyll and Langdale. A strong contrast to this battlemented facade is that provided by the dreary upland hollow lying beyond (Harrison Combe) from which easy slopes fall away to Stake Pass, northwest, pausing in their descent to form the broad plateau of Martcrag Moor.

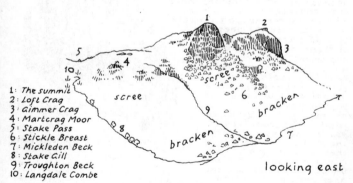

1: The summit
2: Loft Crag
3: Gimmer Crag
4: Martcrag Moor
5: Stake Pass
6: Stickle Breast
7: Mickleden Beck
8: Stake Gill
9: Troughton Beck
10: Langdale Combe

looking east

Thousands of years ago, before the dawn of history, Pike o' Stickle was the scene of an industry the evidences of which have only recently been discovered, and the fell is now established as the country's most important site of stone-axe manufacture by neolithic man. As such it is attracting increasing attention by archaeologists and geologists, but walkers with no expert knowledge of the subject will also find an absorbing interest in a study of the related literature, as yet incomplete, and they may care to combine with their expeditions in this area a search into the dim but fascinating secrets of the past.

The south scree, from Mickleden

The Stone Axe Factory

The intrusion of a narrow vein of a very hard stone in the volcanic rocks of Great Langdale, emerging on the surface along a high-level contour around the head of the valley, provided the material from which the prehistoric natives of the district fashioned their axes. Working sites have been located from Martcrag Moor to Harrison Stickle, but the screes of Pike o' Stickle have yielded the most prolific discoveries, and especially the 'south scree' where hundreds of specimens, originally rejected because of imperfections, have been collected in recent years.

The really remarkable feature is not so much the presence of this particular variety of stone, nor the making of implements from it so long ago; the facts that most tax the imagination are, first, that the primitive inhabitants of Lakeland should have located such an insignificant geological fault and recognised its value, and secondly, that the plentiful evidences of their industry should have remained undisturbed and unnoticed throughout the ages until modern times.

In the rock wall of the south scree is this well-made artificial cave.
Its connection with stone-axe manufacture hereabouts has not yet been accepted authoritatively, although the coincidence seems too great to be denied.
A few feet square, it provides excellent shelter for several persons.

Length 9½"
Width 3"
Maximum Thickness 1½"
Weight 2¼ lbs

Stone axe found on Pike o' Stickle
— a particularly good specimen in the collection of Mr. R.G.Plint, of Kendal

MAP

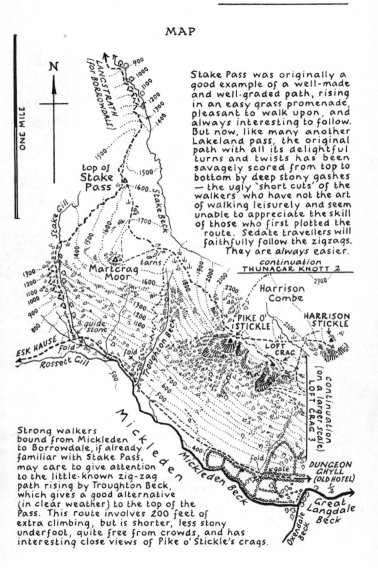

Stake Pass was originally a good example of a well-made and well-graded path, rising in an easy grass promenade, pleasant to walk upon, and always interesting to follow. But now, like many another Lakeland pass, the original path with all its delightful turns and twists has been savagely scored from top to bottom by deep stony gashes — the ugly 'short cuts' of the walkers who have not the art of walking leisurely and seem unable to appreciate the skill of those who first plotted the route. Sedate travellers will faithfully follow the zigzags. They are *always* easier.

Strong walkers bound from Mickleden to Borrowdale, if already familiar with Stake Pass, may care to give attention to the little-known zig-zag path rising by Troughton Beck, which gives a good alternative (in clear weather) to the top of the Pass. This route involves 200 feet of extra climbing, but is shorter, less stony underfoot, quite free from crowds, and has interesting close views of Pike o' Stickle's crags.

ASCENT FROM MICKLEDEN
2000 feet of ascent

3¼ miles via Troughton Beck,
1¾ miles direct (from the
Dungeon Ghyll Old Hotel)

PIKE O' STICKLE

TOP OF STAKE PASS

Martcrag Moor

2000
1800
1700
1600
1500
1400
1300
1200
1100
900
800

cave

In the final gully the best footing is on the east side

scree-run

scree-run

bracken

Initially there is no path by the beck, but one materialises as the ground steepens. It is indistinct on top of the fell.

This path in the strip of bracken between scree-runs has obviously been made by travellers descending at speed; it is not 'stepped' and is of little help in ascent.

sheepfold

STAKE PASS and ESK HAUSE

Troughton Beck

bracken

grass

shallow dry gully

patch of rushes

big boulder

700   800

looking north·north·west

bracken

600   500

400

Mickleden Beck

Mickleden

ruin

gate   DUNGEON GHYLL (OLD HOTEL)

sheepfold

½

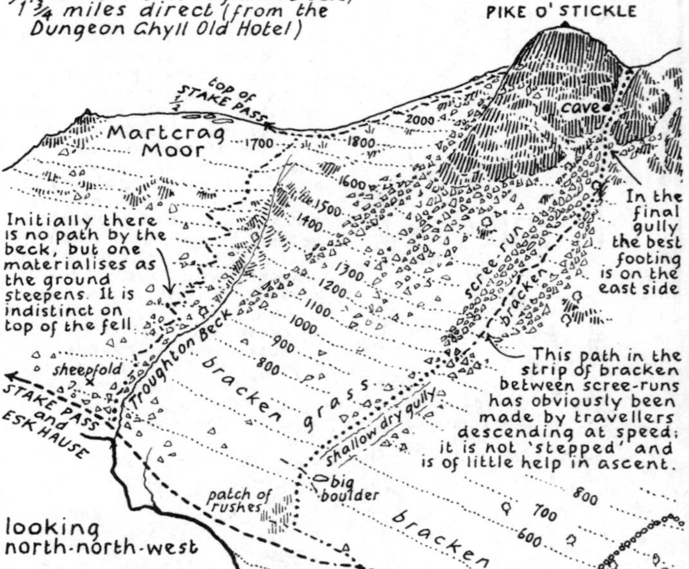

Pike o' Stickle is almost invariably reached from the valley by turning left off the usual Harrison Stickle path at the Thorn Crag *col*, but illustrated here are two other possibilities —
first, via the unfrequented zig-zags climbing the west bank of Troughton Beck, by which the path coming up from the top of Stake Pass may be joined for the summit of the Pike;
second, direct up the south scree, a continuously steep and unpleasant scramble in prickly, unstable scree, and of interest only to searchers after stone axes; the route is dry and dusty but bilberries will be found in season higher up and will seem, by the time they are reached, a greater prize than stone axes to the untrained eye and unlearned mind, which will already have selected and discarded hundreds of likely axes in the splintery stones and debris heaps that litter this desperate climb. In a buttoned-up plastic mac, the ascent is purgatory.

ASCENT FROM THE TOP OF STAKE PASS
800 feet of ascent : 1⅓ miles

PIKE O' STICKLE

looking south·east

The surroundings are dull but interest is sustained by the striking sugarloaf appearance of the Pike, which is no less imposing on this unfamiliar side and makes a worthwhile objective.

The summit is a will-o'-the-wisp on this approach, frequently coming into and vanishing from sight in rather amusing fashion.

Evidences of stone-axe manufacture have been discovered in the upland valley of Stake Beck

Stake Beck

moraines

2200
2100
2000
1900
1800
1700

county boundary

Troughton Beck

tarns   Martcrag Moor

grass

1700

boulders

1600

cairn △

top of
Stake Pass
1576'

BORROWDALE
(STONETHWAITE 4)

GREAT LANGDALE
(DUNGEON GHYLL
OLD HOTEL 3¼)

By a short detour the cairn on Martcrag Moor may be visited. This rocky little top is a commanding viewpoint for the head of Mickleden and it is wonderfully satisfying to lie here in the sunshine and watch parties struggling up Rossett Gill and Stake Pass from the sheepfold far below. Here, too, is one of the most impressive views of Bowfell.

The summit of Pike o' Stickle from the north·west

The cairn on Martcrag Moor

THE SUMMIT

HARRISON STICKLE

The summit is the perfect dome suggested by its appearance from a distance, being circular in plan and bell-shaped, with almost precipitous slopes rising up to it on all sides before finally tapering away gently to the highest point. The top is a pleasant green sward of ample proportions, but exploration is severely restricted by the surrounding crags. Access to the cairn is gained by an easy scramble on the more broken northern slope, this being the only side 'open' to walkers.

DESCENTS :

To Great Langdale : Expert scree-runners will come down the open gully immediately east of the summit-dome and reach the valley-bottom in Mickleden in a matter of minutes, but ordinary mortals will find this route very trying to the temper, although it is probably the safest way in mist and the most sheltered in bad weather. The more usual procedure normally is to join a good path (from Harrison Stickle) at the Thorn Crag col. The route via Troughton Beck has no merits in descent.

1: top of Stake Pass

ignore these paths, which go nowhere in particular.

2 : Harrison Stickle
3 : Loft Crag; Thorn Crag
4 : Mickleden (direct)

To Borrowdale : The path to the top of Stake Pass presents no difficulties in clear weather and must be attempted in mist because there is no other ; take care to start on the right track

RIDGE ROUTE

PIKE O' STICKLE
HARRISON STICKLE
THORN CRAG col
LOFT CRAG
¼ mile

TO LOFT CRAG, 2270'
⅓ mile : E, then SE
100 feet of ascent

At the first depression, follow the less distinct track branching up right: this keeps an interesting course along the ridge

THE VIEW

The view is extensive, especially to the north, although it is interrupted in other directions by nearby higher ground. But the best thing to be seen is below the skyline: the head of Mickleden far beneath, with Bowfell a magnificent object as a background to the picture.

Principal Fells

N

BINSEY
SKIDDAW
CARL SIDE
LONG SIDE
LONSCALE FELL
KNOTT
20 miles
BLENCATHRA
BARF
LORD'S SEAT
CAUSEY PIKE
CATBELLS
15 miles
GRISEDALE PIKE
EEL CRAG
HELVELLYN LOWER MAN
GRANGE FELL
HIGH SEAT
HELVELLYN
GRASMOOR
HIGH SPY
NETHERMOST PIKE
10 miles
MAIDEN MOOR
HIGH RAISE
DOLLYWAGGON PIKE
HIGH STILE
DALE HEAD
SERGEANT'S CRAG
FT SUNDAY CRAG
BRANDRETH
CLARAMARA
FAIRFIELD
GREEN GABLE
THUNACAR
HART CRAG
HART CRAG
GREAT GABLE
PAVEY
GREAT RIGG
DOVE CRAG
KIRK FELL E.
PAVEY
HIGH STREET
GREAT END
THORNTHWAITE CRAG
ESK PIKE
W--SCAFELL PIKE
HARRISON STICKLE-------------E
BOWFELL
SILVER HOW
WANSFELL PIKE
LOFT CRAG
LOUGHRIGG FELL
LINGMOOR FELL
CRINKLE CRAGS
5 miles
GREY FRIAR
COLD PIKE
DOVE CRAG
GREAT CARRS
SWIRL CARRS
WETHERLAM
SILVER HOW
S

Also prominently seen, but not shown on the diagram for lack of space, is Pike o' Blisco across Mickleden in front of the Coniston Fells

Lakes and Tarns

ESE : *Loughrigg Tarn*
ESE : *Elterwater*
SE : *Windermere (upper reach and strip of middle)*
SE : *Lingmoor Tarn*
SE : *Esthwaite Water*
SSE : *Blea Tarn*
WNW : *Nameless tarns on Martcrag Moor*
NNW : *Tarn at Leaves (on Rosthwaite Fell)*

Raven Crag

1520'
approx.

Dale Bottom
●

BLEABERRY
FELL ▲
Smeathwaite
● Bridge

▲
RAVEN CRAG

HIGH ▲
SEAT
● Armboth

MILES

0   1   2   3   4

from the Thirlmere dam

NATURAL FEATURES

Of the many dozens of Raven Crags in Lakeland, best known of all, and the subject of this chapter, is the mighty buttress of grey rock towering above the Thirlmere dam. The vertical face of the crag, now receiving the attention of expert rock-climbers, is a truly formidable object, standing out starkly from a dense surround of plantations.

Raven Crag, which is properly a ridge of High Tove, must have caused problems (left unsolved) for the reservoir engineers because this tremendous barrier of rock turns many streams descending from the central ridge northwards into the Naddle Valley and away from Thirlmere. Oddly, a similar but smaller formation occurs on the opposite side of the dam, where the wooded height of Great How also originally diverted many streams of the Helvellyn mass northwards into St. John's-in-the-Vale — here, however, the engineers captured them by a water-race and turned them into Thirlmere.

North from Raven Crag the ridge is terminated by The Benn, dropping to valley level at Shoulthwaite.

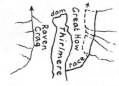

MAP

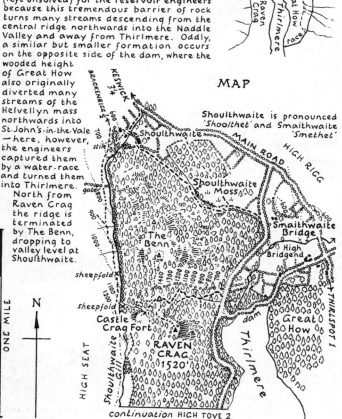

Shoulthwaite is pronounced 'Shoolthet' and Smaithwaite 'Smethet'

continuation HIGH TOVE 2

ASCENT FROM THIRLMERE DAM
950 feet of ascent : 1 mile

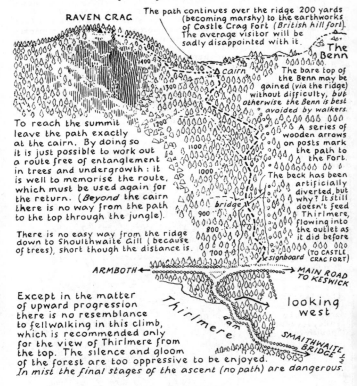

RAVEN CRAG

The path continues over the ridge 200 yards (becoming marshy) to the earthworks of Castle Crag Fort (British hill fort). The average visitor will be sadly disappointed with it.

The Benn

1400

△ cairn

The bare top of the Benn may be gained (via the ridge) without difficulty, but otherwise the Benn is best avoided by walkers.

1300

To reach the summit leave the path exactly at the cairn. By doing so it is just possible to work out a route free of entanglement in trees and undergrowth : it is well to memorise the route, which must be used again for the return. (*Beyond* the cairn there is no way from the path to the top through the jungle).

1200

1100

A series of wooden arrows on posts mark the path to the Fort.

1000

The beck has been artificially diverted, but why? It still doesn't feed Thirlmere, flowing into the outlet as it did before

bridge

900

800

There is no easy way from the ridge down to Shoulthwaite Gill (because of trees), short though the distance is.

700

x signboard

(TO CASTLE CRAG FORT)

ARMBOTH ←

→ MAIN ROAD TO KESWICK

looking west

Except in the matter of upward progression there is no resemblance to fellwalking in this climb, which is recommended only for the view of Thirlmere from the top. The silence and gloom of the forest are too oppressive to be enjoyed.

Thirlmere

dam

SMAITHWAITE BRIDGE ½

In mist the final stages of the ascent (no path) are dangerous.

THE SUMMIT

The summit, of tough heather, is unusual because of its screen of trees. The highest point is a small outcrop of rock, bearing a few stones built into a meagre cairn. A ruined wall crosses the top, a relic of days when sheep lived here — before the growing plantations drove them to other pastures. The summit breaks away suddenly into the most fearful precipice and exploration here is severely restricted. *The only way down is the route used for ascent, not easily located as far as the cairn unless memorised on the way up.*

THE VIEW

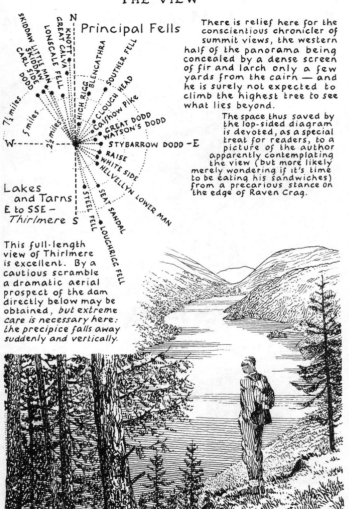

Principal Fells

SKIDDAW
LITTLE MAN
SKIDDAW
CARL SIDE
DODD

SADDLEBACK (BLENCATHRA)
GREAT CALVA
LONSCALE FELL

KNOTT

N

SOUTHER FELL

HIGH RIGG
BLENCATHRA

CLOUGH HEAD

Calfhow Pike

GREAT DODD
WATSON'S DODD

STYBARROW DODD — E

RAISE

WHITE SIDE

HELVELLYN LOWER MAN

SEAT SANDAL

STEEL FELL

LOUGHRIGG FELL

7½ miles

5 miles

2½ miles

W —

Lakes
and Tarns
E to SSE —
Thirlmere S

This full-length view of Thirlmere is excellent. By a cautious scramble a dramatic aerial prospect of the dam directly below may be obtained, *but extreme care is necessary here: the precipice falls away suddenly and vertically.*

There is relief here for the conscientious chronicler of summit views, the western half of the panorama being concealed by a dense screen of fir and larch only a few yards from the cairn — and he is surely not expected to climb the highest tree to see what lies beyond.

The space thus saved by the lop-sided diagram is devoted, as a special treat for readers, to a picture of the author apparently contemplating the view (but more likely merely wondering if it's time to be eating his sandwiches) from a precarious stance on the edge of Raven Crag.

from Great Castle How

HIGH RAISE
▲
▲   ▲ TARN CRAG
SERGEANT MAN
HARRISON ▲
STICKLE   ●   Grasmere
●
Dungeon Ghyll

MILES

0   1   2   3   4

NATURAL FEATURES

Sergeant Man is merely a rocky excrescence at the edge of the broad expanse forming the top of High Raise, but is so prominent an object and offers so compelling a challenge (in these respects being far superior to the summit of High Raise itself) that it is often given preference over the main fell as the target of a day's outing, and for that reason it is deserving of a separate chapter. Behind the abrupt peak, which rises steeply from the basin containing Stickle Tarn, is a hinterland of craggy outcrops and ravines that are rarely visited although yielding, in fact, more interest than the environs of the summit; in particular the area of Fern Gill and Broadstone Head, descending with the county boundary to the valley heads of Wythburn and Far Easedale is fruitful ground for the explorer.

1 : The summit
2 : High Raise
3 : Ridge continuing to Thunacar Knott
4 : Ridge continuing to Blea Rigg
5 : Tarn Crag
6 : Ferngill Crag
7 : Broadstone Head
8 : Belles Knott
9 : Lang Crag
10 : Codale Tarn
11 : Easedale Tarn
12 : Far Easedale

peat hags

bracken

moraines

looking west

MAP

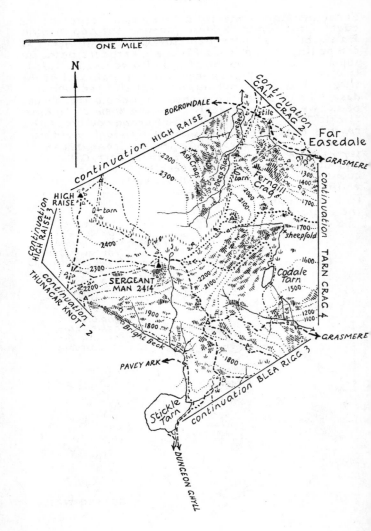

ASCENT FROM DUNGEON GHYLL
2¼ miles : 2200 feet of ascent from the New Hotel

SERGEANT MAN

2300
2200
2100
2000
1900
1800
1700
1600

PAVEY ARK

→ BLEA RIGG
→ BLEA RIGG

Here the path passes a 50-foot slab set at an easy inclination (cairn in the middle of it) giving a rare opportunity for rock-walking.

Here the ridge is gained amid a profusion of cairns. This is a well-known 'crossroads'.

Here the path forks among stones below a craggy slope, *indistinctly*. The Sergeant Man branch is identified by a small walled enclosure only 10 yards past the fork

Stickle Tarn

1600
1500

Tarn Crag — Sergeant Man comes into view

ruin

1400
1300
1200
1100
1000
900
800

Of the two main paths alongside Mill Gill (one on each side) the left is the one more often used, the other (east bank) has a special attraction almost unique on Lakeland paths: a rock stairway requiring continuous hand-and-foot climbing for a considerable distance up the lower buttress of Tarn Crag. This interesting route may be avoided by following the stream closely.

The zigzag alternative (the *original* path) is on grass, and a pleasant relief from the many stones hereabouts. It diverges a few yards short of the first stream *after* the sheepfold and is easily missed: there is a cairn.

Miller Crag

ruined sheepfold

700
600
500
400
300

OLD HOTEL 3

OLD HOTEL 4

Millbeck

New Hotel

CHAPEL STILE 2

Dungeon Ghyll

looking north

If Mill Gill is in spate it is better to gain the east bank at once by using the footbridge in the little enclosure behind the hotel and following the path from Millbeck Farm

A popular walk, with gill, tarn and rock scenery of the highest order and good views all the way.

ASCENT FROM GRASMERE
2200 feet of ascent : 4 miles

SERGEANT MAN

Here the path passes a 50-foot rock slab with a cairn oddly set in the middle. Its easy gradient makes it climbable by *walking*.

Prominent cairn visible from hut

Here the ridge is gained amid a profusion of cairns. This is a well-known 'crossroads.' Routes from Dungeon Ghyll and Blea Rigg to Sergeant Man join in at this point.

← BLEA RIGG

grass

Codale Tarn

The path becomes a scramble on easy rock as it skirts the edge of the crags above point marked A.

Belles Knott

Blea Crag

Eagle Crag

'A' indicates the start of the variation by Codale Tarn, illustrated opposite.

old tarn bed

Black slime is experienced at its blackest and slimiest at frequent intervals on the path alongside Easedale Tarn and beyond, but conditions underfoot improve as soon as the old tarn is passed.

The summit of Sergeant Man cannot be seen from the hut and does not come into sight until the final stages of the climb.

Easedale Tarn   × sheepfold

old refreshment hut

looking west

Blea Crag and Eagle Crag form an imposing precipice on the left but the dominating feature on the march up the valley is the peak of Belles Knott, which assumes a striking appearance from the path as it is approached.

This is the most direct and the quickest route. From Easedale Tarn the path follows the main feeder almost to its source before slanting up to the ridge. The route is too deeply enclosed to be attractive, although there are several interesting features. If returning to Grasmere, the more exhilarating Blea Rigg ridge is a better route of descent than the one illustrated above.

ASCENT FROM GRASMERE
(VARIATION BY CODALE TARN)
2200 feet of ascent : 4¼ miles

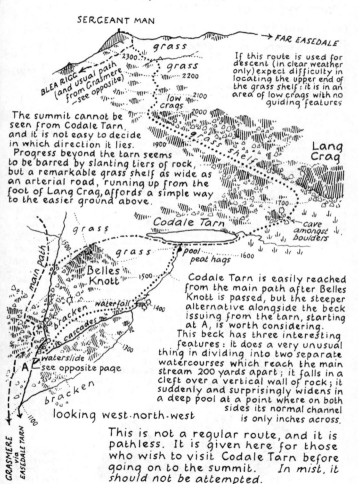

SERGEANT MAN

→ FAR EASEDALE

grass

BLEA RIGG ← *(and usual path from Grasmere — see opposite)*

2300

grass

2200

low crags

2100

2000

1900

grass shelf

Lang Crag

1700

If this route is used for descent (in clear weather only) expect difficulty in locating the upper end of the grass shelf: it is in an area of low crags with no guiding features

The summit cannot be seen from Codale Tarn, and it is not easy to decide in which direction it lies. Progress beyond the tarn seems to be barred by slanting tiers of rock, but a remarkable grass shelf as wide as an arterial road, running up from the foot of Lang Crag, affords a simple way to the easier ground above.

cave amongst boulders

Codale Tarn

grass

1500

grass

main path

pool peat hags

1600

Belles Knott

1500

waterfall

1400

cascades

bracken

1300

A

waterslide see opposite page

bracken

1100

looking west·north·west

Codale Tarn is easily reached from the main path after Belles Knott is passed, but the steeper alternative alongside the beck issuing from the tarn, starting at A, is worth considering. This beck has three interesting features: it does a very unusual thing in dividing into two separate watercourses which reach the main stream 200 yards apart; it falls in a cleft over a vertical wall of rock; it suddenly and surprisingly widens in a deep pool at a point where on both sides its normal channel is only inches across.

GRASMERE via EASEDALE TARN

This is not a regular route, and it is pathless. It is given here for those who wish to visit Codale Tarn before going on to the summit. In mist, it should not be attempted.

ASCENT FROM THE HEAD OF FAR EASEDALE
(reached from GRASMERE or WYTHBURN)
from Grasmere : 2200 feet of ascent : 5½ miles
from Wythburn : 1850 feet of ascent : 5 miles

For a diagram of the route to the head of Far Easedale from Grasmere, see Calf Crag 3; from Wythburn, see Calf Crag 5.

SERGEANT MAN

HIGH RAISE

grass

This is the small peak that appears from Grasmere to be the summit of the fell.

Note in these peat hags an unusual content of decayed timber not yet decomposed. This suggests that the slopes were wooded in comparatively recent times (altitude 1650')

2300
2200
2100
2000
1900
1800
1700

old fence
tarn
tarns
tarn
Deep Slack
CRAG
Birks
waterfalls
Mere Beck
Broadstone Head

Far Easedale

stile
peat hags
GRASMERE
WYTHBURN
BORROWDALE

looking south

The purist who insists on keeping strictly to the line of the fence will enjoy some easy scrambling. He will also find himself waist-deep in water at one point where the fence originally made a beeline across the corner of a tarn; incidentally, this is an attractive sheet of water (viewed from *terra firma*) in rocky surroundings.

Observant walkers will readily appreciate that it is not really necessary to climb the stile at the head of Far Easedale, the fence on both sides of it having vanished completely.

This route merits no preference over others except that it is a quiet and 'unknown' way to the top — a consideration on bank holidays; and this is especially so if the start be arranged from Wythburn. There is no path on the section illustrated. The fence, now derelict, marks the boundary between Cumberland and Westmorland.

The small peak prominently seen from Grasmere

THE SUMMIT

The stones around the cairn have been scratched white by the nailed boots of visitors, testifying to the popularity of this summit. Southwards the ground falls away steeply and roughly, and it is usual to leave the cairn northwards, where a spiny little ridge descends easily to a network of paths. There is swampy ground on the top of the fell, and many small tarns. Sergeant Man is distinctive in having a stream within a furlong of the cairn, a point for specialists in mountain bivouacs to note. The well-built cairn is a prominent landmark.

DESCENTS : The usual way off the top is by the Blea Rigg path. In mist, the Blea Rigg path is best, being well-cairned although indistinct in places, if Grasmere or Langdale is the destination. For Borrowdale or Wythburn, strike north to the old fence (250 yards) and follow it left over High Raise to Greenup Edge.

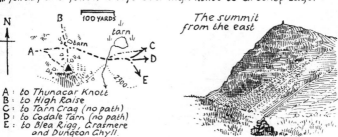

A : to Thunacar Knott
B : to High Raise
C : to Tarn Crag (no path)
D : to Codale Tarn (no path)
E : to Blea Rigg, Grasmere and Dungeon Ghyll.

The summit from the east

THE VIEW

The fine view is robbed of all-round excellence only by the tedious and extensive slopes of High Raise between west and north. It is a view of mountains almost exclusively, not of valleys. The most striking scene is that southwards, where Pavey Ark and Harrison Stickle rise starkly against a background formed by the Coniston Fells.

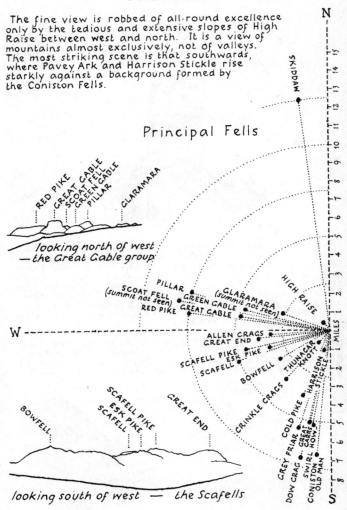

Principal Fells

looking north of west — the Great Gable group

looking south of west — the Scafells

THE VIEW

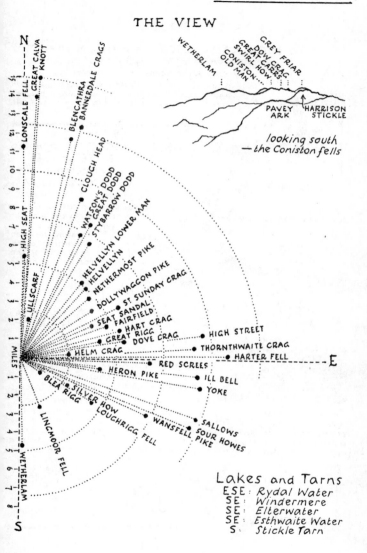

looking south
— the Coniston fells

Lakes and Tarns
ESE: Rydal Water
SE: Windermere
SE: Elterwater
SE: Esthwaite Water
S: Stickle Tarn

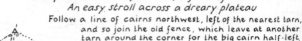

RIDGE ROUTES

To HIGH RAISE, 2500' : ½ mile : N, then NW
Depression at 2370' : 140 feet of ascent
An easy stroll across a dreary plateau
Follow a line of cairns northwest, left of the nearest tarn, and so join the old fence, which leave at another tarn around the corner for the big cairn half-left.

To BLEA RIGG, 1776' : 1½ miles
N, then E, SSE and SE
Minor depressions only
100 feet of ascent
An easy, interesting walk
A profusion of cairns at the base of a low crag marks the junction of paths. Keep straight on here trending to the left side of the broad ridge ahead

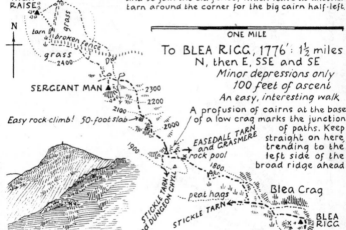

The summit from the rock slab

To TARN CRAG, 1801' : 1¼ miles
NE, then E
Slight depressions : 100 feet of ascent
An interesting test in route-finding.

There is no path. The difficulty is to find the line of cairns leading away from the fence. The point occurs near two tarns *before* the prominent rocky peak is reached and the route descends alongside a runnel in the grass at first. The cairns are continuous to the end of the wide ridge, where the summit of Tarn Crag is near on the left.

This is a route for clear weather only

Belles Knott, the 'Matterhorn' of Easedale

This sharp peak is a prominent feature in the early stages of the walk by the path from Easedale Tarn to Dungeon Ghyll.   Its shapeliness diminishes as the path is ascended, however, and the summit is finally seen to be approachable from behind by a simple grass promenade at a very easy gradient. Codale Tarn is nearby.

Sergeant's Crag

1873'

- Rosthwaite
- Stonethwaite
- ▲ EAGLE CRAG
- ▲ SERGEANT'S CRAG
- ▲ HIGH RAISE

MILES
0 1 2 3

from Eagle Crag

NATURAL FEATURES

The extensive north-western slopes of High Raise descend gradually and uneventfully at first, with nothing of interest to show; and then, after some hesitation, rise sharply to the walled summit of Sergeant's Crag before plunging precipitously, without further delay, to Langstrath far below. The change is sudden and the contrast complete, for High Raise is smooth and grassy for the most part, Sergeant's Crag is all rock and rough fell. The main crag, overlooking the valley, is a sheer wall of rock split by two gullies of which the more prominent is, or was before fashions changed, a favourite resort of climbers. The Langstrath slopes are very steep everywhere, and a tumble of fallen blocks obstructs easy passage of the popular path to Stake Pass along the base — one huge boulder in particular, Blea Rock, crowning a little rise, is a conspicuous landmark here.

Blackmoss Pot (or Blackmer Pot) Here Langstrath Beck forms a deep, silent pool in a rocky gorge, a picturesque scene, and one that should be visited by all who pass along the valley. The Pot cannot be seen from the path although quite near. It is located where the wall comes down the fellside to the beck and crosses it.

Blea Rock (also known as Cash Rock)

Sergeant's Crag 3

MAP

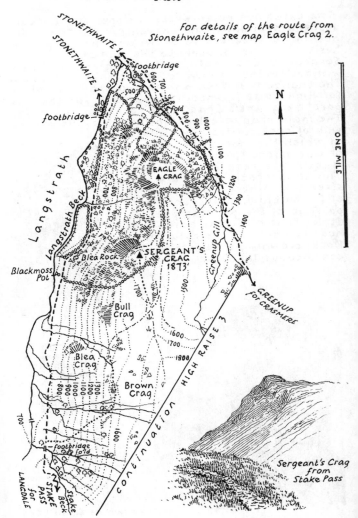

For details of the route from
Stonethwaite, see map Eagle Crag 2.

STONETHWAITE 1

STONETHWAITE 1

footbridge

footbridge

N

ONE MILE

Langstrath

Langstrath Beck

EAGLE CRAG

Fold

Greenup Gill

GREENUP
for GRASMERE

Blea Rock

SERGEANT'S
CRAG
1873'

Blackmoss
Pot

Bull
Crag

Blea
Crag

Brown
Crag

continuation HIGH RAISE 3

footbridge fold

STAKE PASS
for LANGDALE

Stake Beck

Sergeant's Crag
from
Stake Pass

ASCENT FROM STONETHWAITE
1600 feet of ascent
4½ miles by the route illustrated

HIGH RAISE

Greenup Edge

SERGEANT'S CRAG

tor

shepherd's track

Brown Crag

STAKE PASS

EAGLE CRAG

Bull Crag

1500
1400
1300

Blea Crag

1200
1100
1000
900
800

Blea Rock

bracken

Blackmoss Pot

GREENUP GILL

EAGLE CRAG (ROUTE A)

GREENUP CRAG and EAGLE CRAG (ROUTE B)

700
600
500

Langstrath Beck

Langstrath

footbridge

Galleny Force

STONETHWAITE BECK

GREENUP

ROSTHWAITE (path) ↑

ROSTHWAITE (road) ↑

Continue along Langstrath for a mile beyond Blackmoss Pot, as far as the footbridge at the foot of Stake Pass; here turn up grass slopes on the left (no path), aiming for Brown Crag. Sergeant's Crag is in view from the top of Brown Crag: either make a beeline for it or pick up a useful track below the intervening rock tor. Finally, a wall must be surmounted to gain the summit

This route is circuitous but easy: a direct ascent of the Langstrath face, evading the rim of crags, is just possible but too rough on the upper part to be recommended.
The best way of all, however, is to climb Eagle Crag first, and proceed along the ridge (see Eagle Crag 3).

Stonethwaite   Leave the hamlet by the lane (or, more pleasantly, by the field-path), not by the Greenup track over the bridge.

Langstrath is a fine valley and this route introduces it nicely, while shirking the difficulties of direct ascent. Sergeant's Crag is dangerous in mist.

looking south-east

THE SUMMIT

The rocky, heathery top within the wall is a pleasant contrast to the dull grassland outside it, and if there is no apprehension about the weather the halt here will be enjoyed. The cairn stands on a comfortable rock platform, one buttressing wall of which has splintered recently, to reveal the light colour and texture of the unweathered stone. If it is desired to locate the top exit of Sergeant's Crag Gully, this diagram shows the way to it — *but descents here will end fatally.* ▍*In bad weather, go down easy* ▍*slopes eastwards (over the wall)* to Greenup Gill.

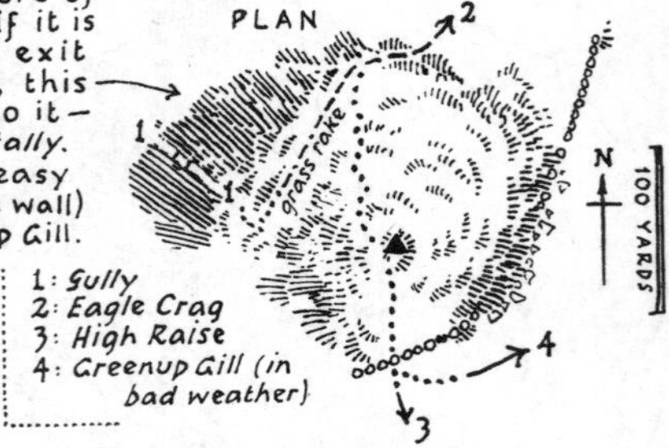

PLAN

grass rake

100 YARDS

1: Gully
2: Eagle Crag
3: High Raise
4: Greenup Gill (in bad weather)

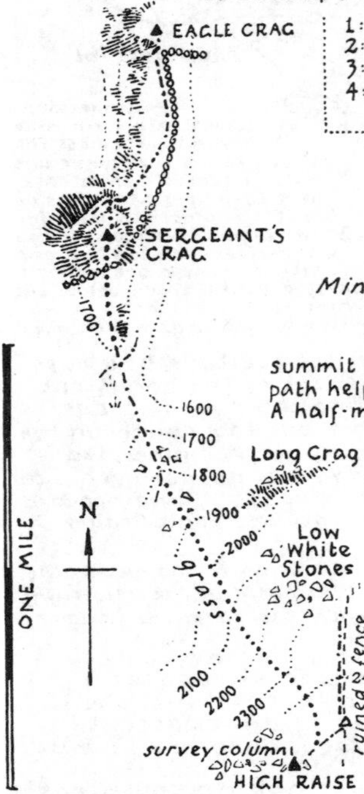

▲ EAGLE CRAG

▲ SERGEANT'S CRAG

1700
1600
1700
1800
Long Crag
1900
2000
Low White Stones
2100
2200
2300
2400
survey column
ruined fence
HIGH RAISE

ONE MILE

RIDGE ROUTES

TO EAGLE CRAG, 1650':
½ mile : NNE, then N
Minor depressions : 50 feet of ascent
No difficulties

There is no trouble in getting off the summit in the direction of Eagle Crag; a short path helps. Incline to the wall; do not cross it. A half-minute's scramble near the wall-corner leads on to Eagle Crag.

TO HIGH RAISE, 2500':
1½ miles : SSE :
Depression at 1650':
850 feet of ascent
An easy, tedious climb on grass

Cross the summit-wall without dislodging stones and then aim in a slight curve for the lengthy slopes ahead. A sketchy track traverses the depression, but no path is available for the grassy climb beyond. Keep well to the right of Long Crag.

THE VIEW

There is a splendid prospect up Langstrath to Bowfell and Esk Pike. Nearer, High Raise and Ullscarf form a vast, high screen eastwards, displaying little of interest, but elsewhere the view is fairly good, with many familiar 'tops' peeping over Glaramara.

Principal Fells

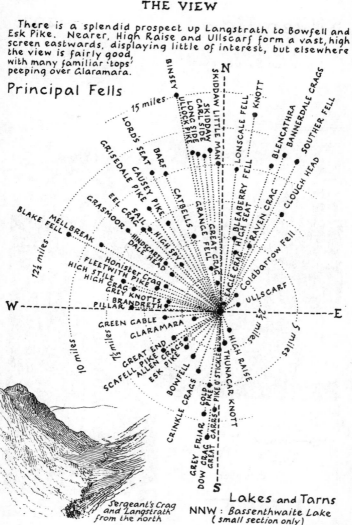

Sergeant's Crag and Langstrath from the north

Lakes and Tarns

NNW : Bassenthwaite Lake
(small section only)

Silver How

1292'

'Silver Howe' on
Ordnance Survey maps

Grasmere ●

SILVER HOW ▲

Chapel ● Stile

LOUGHRIGG ▲ FELL

Elterwater ●

MILES
0 1 2 3 4

from Loughrigg Terrace

NATURAL FEATURES

A lovely name for a lovely fell: Silver How is delightful. Not because the summit is remarkable, except for the view; the grassy top is, indeed, the least of its attractions. It is the rough slopes that delight the eye, especially on the Grasmere side, for the intermingling of crag and conifer, juniper and bracken, is landscape artistry at its best. A wealth of timber adorns the lower slopes and trees persist into the zone of crags fringing the summit. Fine waterfalls are another characteristic, though none is well known: Blindtarn Gill, Wray Gill, and Meg's Gill, the latter the best, all have spectacular cataracts.

Silver How is a prominent height on the wide and broken ridge that may be said to start with Loughrigg Fell and continue, dividing Langdale and Easedale, to High Raise, the highest point.

looking north-west

1: The summit
2: Ridge continuing to Loughrigg Fell
3: Red Bank
4: Spedding Crag
5: Raven Crag
6: Megs Gill
7: Wray Gill
8: Blindtarn Gill
9: Easedale
10: Great Langdale
11: Grasmere
12: River Rothay

Passes between Grasmere and Great Langdale:
A: via Megs Gill
B: via Hunting Stile
C: via Red Bank

MAP

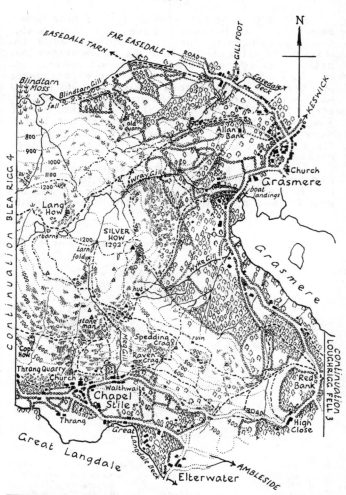

ONE MILE

ASCENT FROM GRASMERE
1100 feet of ascent : 1½ miles

SILVER HOW
The Langdale edge
BLEA RIGG
Lang How
CHAPEL STILE
1200
1100 plateau
shooting hut (ruin)
scree gully
1000
juniper and bracken
bracken slope
grass
well-defined zone of juniper (800'-1000')
900
1000
boulders
juniper
fall
800
private grounds and plantations
falls
700
gate
fall
600
500
400
Forget about Silver How for a few minutes here and halt to admire the beautiful specimen trees in these lower pastures
700
This lane is overgrown and the path escapes from it to run outside the wall
500
Score Crag
LANGDALE via RED BANK
400
(farm)
Grasmere
boat landings
Allan Bank was a temporary residence of Wordsworth (1808-1811)
bridge (1922)
Second gate beyond bridge gives access to lane between walls
300
Allan Bank
This is the usual route
nursery
AMBLESIDE 4
gate
drive cart track
Red Lion studio
Church
EASEDALE
Grasmere
looking south-west
KESWICK

Two routes are given, both supremely beautiful walks, with a rough variation by Wray Gill if desired. The views are charming. Alternatively, the summit may be reached from any of the ridge-passes to Langdale.

ASCENT FROM ELTERWATER
1200 feet of ascent : 2¼ miles

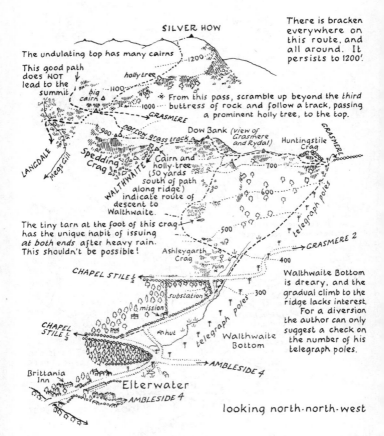

SILVER HOW

The undulating top has many cairns

There is bracken everywhere on this route, and all around. It persists to 1200'.

This good path does NOT lead to the summit

*From this pass, scramble up beyond the *third* buttress of rock and follow a track, passing a prominent holly tree, to the top.

holly tree

1200

1100

big cairn

1000

GRASMERE

Dow Bank *(view of Grasmere and Rydal)*

900

rotten grass track

Huntingstile Crag

700

LANGDALE

Negs Gill

Spedding Crag

WALTHWAITE

Cairn and holly-tree (50 yards south of path along ridge) indicate route of descent to Walthwaite.

600

telegraph poles

500

The tiny tarn at the foot of this crag has the unique habit of issuing *at both ends* after heavy rain. This shouldn't be possible!

Ashleygarth Crag

ruin

GRASMERE 2

400

CHAPEL STILE ½

substation

mission

300

Walthwaite Bottom is dreary, and the gradual climb to the ridge lacks interest. For a diversion the author can only suggest a check on the number of his telegraph poles.

CHAPEL STILE ½

hut

telegraph poles

Walthwaite Bottom

AMBLESIDE 4

Brittania Inn

Elterwater

AMBLESIDE 4

looking north·north·west

After a dull start, interest quickens when the ridge is reached (at either of the points indicated) and the view opens out over Grasmere; thereafter the walk increases in beauty. Winter colourings are very good.

ASCENT FROM CHAPEL STILE
1050 feet of ascent : 1¼ miles

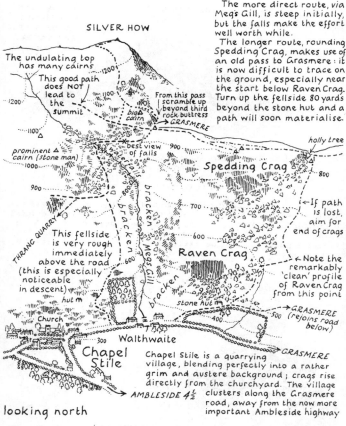

SILVER HOW

The undulating top has many cairns

This good path does NOT lead to the summit

1200

1100

From this pass scramble up beyond third rock buttress

big cairn

GRASMERE

prominent △ cairn (stone man)

1000

900

best view of falls

holly tree

Spedding Crag

800

THRANG QUARRY

This fellside is very rough immediately above the road (this is especially noticeable in descent)

700

600

If path is lost, aim for end of crags

Raven Crag

← Note the remarkable 'clean' profile of Raven Crag from this point

hut

stone hut

GRASMERE (rejoins road below)

Church

400

500

Walthwaite

Chapel Stile

300

Chapel Stile is a quarrying village, blending perfectly into a rather grim and austere background; crags rise directly from the churchyard. The village clusters along the Grasmere road, away from the now more important Ambleside highway

GRASMERE

AMBLESIDE 4½

The more direct route, via Meg's Gill, is steep initially, but the falls make the effort well worth while.

The longer route, rounding Spedding Crag, makes use of an old pass to Grasmere: it is now difficult to trace on the ground, especially near the start below Raven Crag. Turn up the fellside 80 yards beyond the stone hut and a path will soon materialise.

looking north

Silver How displays its finest features to Grasmere and turns a comparatively dowdy back to Langdale; nevertheless the short climb is attractive and the views when the ridge is reached are very charming.

THE SUMMIT

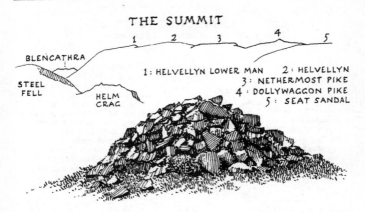

1: HELVELLYN LOWER MAN
2: HELVELLYN
3: NETHERMOST PIKE
4: DOLLYWAGGON PIKE
5: SEAT SANDAL

BLENCATHRA
STEEL FELL
HELM CRAG

The top of the fell is extensive and forms several rounded elevations, most of them cairned, but the actual summit is conspicuously situated above the steep Grasmere face. The paths across the top are little better than narrow sheep-tracks in the grass.

DESCENTS: Commence all descents from the small depression 100 yards west-south-west, turning right for Grasmere and left for Langdale via Meg's Gill. Do not attempt descents *directly* to Grasmere: a wall of crags lies below the summit on this side. *In mist* the paths will not be easy to follow; if they are lost in the early stages keep on in the same direction and they will re-appear.

The stone man above Meg's Gill

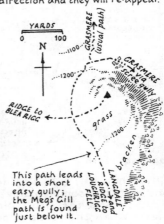

YARDS
0   100

N

1100
1200

GRASMERE (usual path)

GRASMERE via SCREE GULLY

RIDGE to BLEA RIGG ←

grass

1200

bracken

LANGDALE via LOUGHRIGG FELL

This path leads into a short easy gully; the Meg's Gill path is found just below it.

THE VIEW

The vale and village of Grasmere, seen in great detail, take pride of place in a very pleasing view, rich in lake scenery. There is good contrast between the sylvan beauty of the valleys of the Rothay and Brathay and the stark outline of the Coniston and Langdale fells.

This is probably as good a place as any for a newcomer to the district to appreciate its variety and unique charm.

Principal Fells

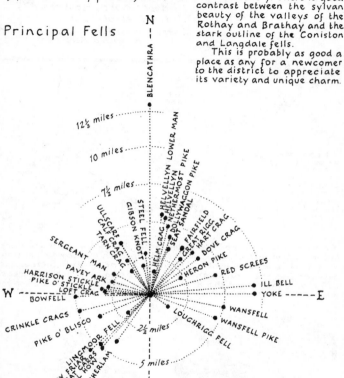

Lakes and Tarns

E: *Grasmere*
E: *Rydal Water*
SE: *Loughrigg Tarn*
SE: *Windermere (upper reach)*
S: *Coniston Water (small part)*

Walk 50 yards south of the cairn for a view of *Elterwater* (SSE)

RIDGE ROUTE

To LOUGHRIGG FELL, 1101′ : 2½ miles
S, then ESE, E and SE
Several depressions ; main one 475′
850 feet of ascent
A very beautiful and easy walk,
finishing with a steep climb

ONE MILE

SILVER HOW ▲

BLEA RIGG

LANGDALE

GRASMERE

Spedding Crag

WALTHWAITE

Dow Bank

A branch path detours to two cairns on Spedding Crag, where there is a striking birds-eye view of Chapel Stile and Walthwaite

Dow Bank is the most prominent rise on the ridge

Cairn on rocky mound – viewpoint for Rydal and Grasmere

ruin

line of telegraph poles

ELTERWATER

ELTERWATER (road)

GRASMERE (road)

Red Bank

Loughrigg Terrace

GRASMERE

AMBLESIDE (road)

LOUGHRIGG FELL ▲

On merit, this should be a well-blazed route, for there are few more beautiful and interesting, but in fact for much of the way a narrow grass trod is the only guide. The views are delightful. Three passes between Grasmere and Langdale are crossed, the first the Meg's Gill route, the second the Hunting Stile route, and the well-known Red Bank road is the third. There should be no difficulty in mist.

Meg's Gill

Cairn on the ridge overlooking Elterwater

RIDGE ROUTE

To BLEA RIGG, 1776': 2 miles
W, then WNW and N
A succession of little ups and downs
650 feet of ascent

Great Castle How ← small rock summit, reached by a detour; fine view of upper Easedale and Sergeant Man.

quartz stones

BLEA RIGG

shelter

1600

tarns

Little Castle How

1400

1300

Watch carefully for the final sharp turn to the right (look for cairns)

1500

Much of the pleasure of this easy and charming walk is derived from following the vagaries of the indistinct path

N

shelter
fold

good viewpoint for Great Langdale

GREAT LANGDALE

1300

1200

Lang How

GRASMERE

SILVER HOW

1200

The half-way shelter (above the Langdale descent) is not for the squeamish.

tarns

tarn

1200
1100

ONE MILE

Langdale Pikes
from the tarns
below Lang How

Steel Fell

1811'

Wythburn
ULLSCARF
CALF CRAG
STEEL FELL
HIGH RAISE
HELM CRAG
Grasmere

MILES
0 1 2 3 4

from Helm Crag

NATURAL FEATURES

Travellers north on the main road over Dunmail Raise are accompanied on the west side soon after leaving Town Head, Grasmere, by a rising ridge of high ground that culminates in a formidable wall of rough fell overlooking the pass itself and then falls abruptly to valley-level before Thirlmere is reached. This familiar height is Steel Fell. It stands on a triangular base, being bounded on the other two sides by the deep troughs of Greenburn and Wythburn,* which are separated by a ridge that forms Steel Fell's only high link with other fells. There is much craggy ground on all flanks. Moraines are in evidence on the easier southern slopes below Dunmail Raise and in the secluded valley of Greenburn, which has other interesting geographical features also.

   * The Scottish influence in the naming of *becks* as *burns* hereabouts is interesting. It occurs again on the west side of Ullswater in the naming of *dales* as *glens*, but rarely elsewhere in the district.

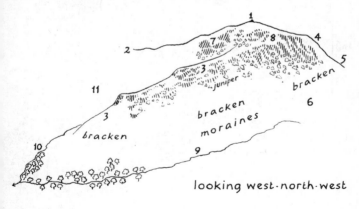

looking west·north·west

1 : The summit   2 : Ridge continuing to Calf Crag
3 : South-east ridge   4 : North ridge
5 : Steel End   6 : Dunmail Raise
7 : Blakerigg Crag   8 : Ash Crags
9 : Raise Beck   10 : Green Burn
11 : The Greenburn Valley

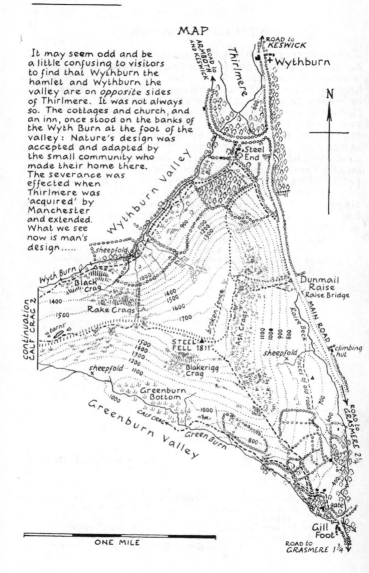

MAP

It may seem odd and be a little confusing to visitors to find that Wythburn the hamlet and Wythburn the valley are on *opposite* sides of Thirlmere. It was not always so. The cottages and church, and an inn, once stood on the banks of the Wyth Burn at the foot of the valley: Nature's design was accepted and adapted by the small community who made their home there. The severance was effected when Thirlmere was 'acquired' by Manchester and extended. What we see now is man's design.....

ROAD to ARMBOTH and KESWICK

ROAD to KESWICK

Thirlmere

✝ Wythburn

N

Steel End

Wythburn Valley

Wyth Burn

Wyth Burn

Black Crag

sheepfold

Rake Crags

Continuation CALF CRAG 2

tarns

1400

1500

1500

1400

1300

1200

STEEL FELL 1811

Blakerigg Crag

sheepfold

1100

Greenburn Bottom

CALF CRAG

1000

Greenburn Valley

1000

900

1000

1100

1200

1300

1400

1500

1600

1700

broken fence

Ash Crags

Green Burn

800

Dunmail Raise

Raise Bridge

MAIN ROAD

Raise Beck

sheepfold

1000

900

800

climbing hut

traces of old road

700

ROAD to GRASMERE 2¼

gate

Gill Foot

ROAD to GRASMERE 1¾

ONE MILE

ASCENT FROM GRASMERE
1650 feet of ascent : 3¼ miles from Grasmere Church

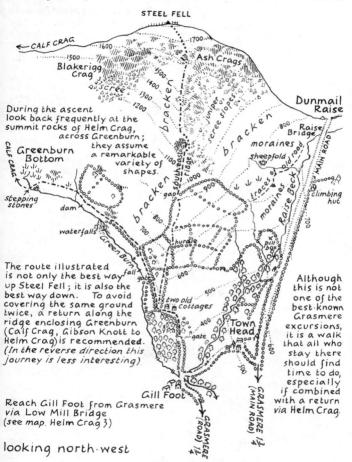

STEEL FELL

← CALF CRAG — 1600 — 1700

Ash Crags

— 1500 —
Blakerigg
Crag

scree — 1500 — 1400 — 1300 — 1200

Dunmail
Raise

During the ascent
look back frequently at the
summit rocks of Helm Crag,
across Greenburn;
they assume
a remarkable
variety of
shapes.

Juniper

scree slopes

bracken

800
Raise
Bridge
moraines
sheepfold

MAIN ROAD

Greenburn
Bottom

CALF CRAG

stepping
stones

dam

waterfalls

Green Burn

bracken

— 1100 —

— 1000 —

gap

900

800

700

hurdle

600

1000

900

traces

moraines

Raise Beck

climbing
hut

800

700

The route illustrated
is not only the best way
up Steel Fell; it is also the
best way down. To avoid
covering the same ground
twice, a return along the
ridge enclosing Greenburn
(Calf Crag, Gibson Knott to
Helm Crag) is recommended.
(In the reverse direction this
journey is less interesting).

fall

gate

500

two old
cottages

400

gate

Town
Head

Although
this is not
one of the
best-known
Grasmere
excursions,
it is a walk
that all who
stay there
should find
time to do,
especially
if combined
with a return
via Helm Crag.

Gill Foot

GRASMERE
(ROAD) 1¼

GRASMERE 1½
(MAIN ROAD)

Reach Gill Foot from Grasmere
via Low Mill Bridge
(see map. Helm Crag 3)

looking north-west

The approach is pleasant and the climbing along
the mile of ascending ridge is very enjoyable, the
slope being well-graded and of good dry turf.

ASCENT FROM WYTHBURN
1250 feet of ascent : 2 miles from Wythburn Church

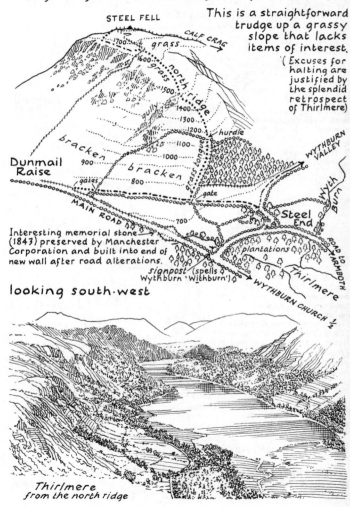

This is a straightforward trudge up a grassy slope that lacks items of interest.

(Excuses for halting are justified by the splendid retrospect of Thirlmere)

STEEL FELL

CALF CRAG

700 grass

1600 grass

north ridge

1500

gully

1400

1300

1200 hurdle

1100

grass tongue

1000

bracken

bracken

900

800

gates

gate

Dunmail Raise

MAIN ROAD

700

WYTHBURN VALLEY

Wyth Burn

Steel End

ROAD TO ARMBOTH

plantations

Thirlmere

Interesting memorial stone (1843) preserved by Manchester Corporation and built into end of new wall after road alterations.

signpost (spells Wythburn 'Withburn')

WYTHBURN CHURCH ½

looking south-west

Thirlmere
from the north ridge

ASCENT FROM DUNMAIL RAISE
1050 feet of ascent : 1 mile

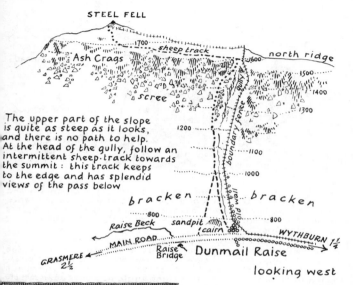

STEEL FELL

1700 — sheep track

Ash Crags

north ridge

1600

1500

1400

1300

scree

The upper part of the slope is quite as steep as it looks, and there is no path to help. At the head of the gully, follow an intermittent sheep-track towards the summit : this track keeps to the edge and has splendid views of the pass below

1200

boundary fence & gully

1100

1000

old wall

bracken   bracken

800   800

Raise Beck   sandpit   cairn

WYTHBURN 1½

MAIN ROAD   Dunmail Raise

GRASMERE 2½   Raise Bridge

looking west

looking along Raise Beck to Fairfield from the top of the gully above Dunmail Raise.

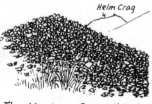

Helm Crag

The old cairn on Dunmail Raise — reputed to mark the site of burial of Dunmail, the last king of Cumberland, 945 A.D.

THE SUMMIT

DOLLYWAGGON PIKE
St SUNDAY CRAG
Deepdale House
Cofa Pike
FAIRFIELD
SEAT SANDAL

A heap of heavy red stones forms a colourful cairn on the highest part of the fell alongside the County boundary fence, which is now in disrepair. Several small tarns lie around, like an untidy and unattractive necklace, in the depressions of the undulating top.

DESCENTS : For Grasmere direct, proceed in the direction of Heron Pike, south-east, until, from the brink of a steep edge, the south ridge is seen below; gain this by an old zig-zag path. For Wythburn, follow the fence, east turning north, for about half a mile, where it forms a right angle and goes down steeply to Dunmail Raise; a pleasanter way down is afforded by the grassy ridge *beyond* the right angle, descending to Steel End.

In mist, it is well to bear in mind that the summit is ringed by crags, and that the fence is an infallible guide to the road at Dunmail Raise, where the only hazards are borne on wheels.

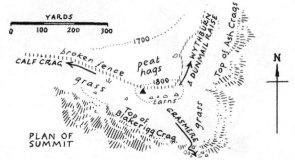

YARDS
0   100   200   300

1700

broken fence
CALF CRAG
peat hags
WYTHBURN
DUNMAIL RAISE
Top of Ash Crags
grass
1800
GRASMERE
grass
tarns
Top of Blakerigg Crag

N

PLAN OF SUMMIT

THE VIEW

Principal Fells

Glaramara and Great Gable, with the Ennerdale face of the latter seen in profile, appear over the Greenup depression.

The view of Grasmere is largely obstructed by Helm Crag, and the best scene unfolds to the north, where the noble Blencathra is a background to Thirlmere. To the southwest, lateral ridges rise one behind another to the skyline of the Coniston fells, all of them being of strikingly serrated appearance of Cuillin-like quality.

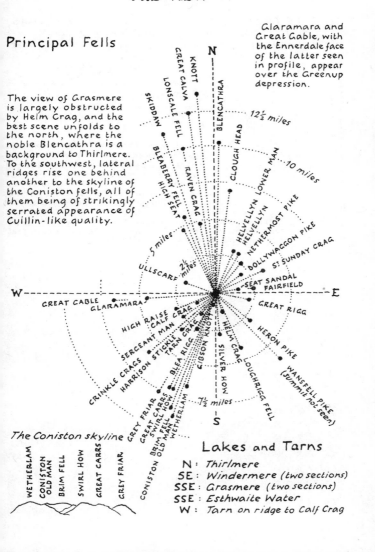

The Coniston skyline

WETHERLAM
CONISTON OLD MAN
BRIM FELL
SWIRL HOW
GREAT CARRS
GREY FRIAR

Lakes and Tarns

N : Thirlmere
SE : Windermere (two sections)
SSE : Grasmere (two sections)
SSE : Esthwaite Water
W : Tarn on ridge to Calf Crag

RIDGE ROUTE

To CALF CRAG, 1762' : 1½ miles : WNW, then W curving S.
Main depression at 1535' : 300 feet of ascent
An easy walk, with fence as guide, but very marshy in places

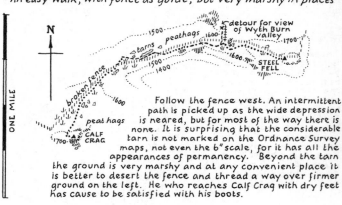

Follow the fence west. An intermittent path is picked up as the wide depression is neared, but for most of the way there is none. It is surprising that the considerable tarn is not marked on the Ordnance Survey maps, not even the 6" scale, for it has all the appearances of permanency. Beyond the tarn the ground is very marshy and at any convenient place it is better to desert the fence and thread a way over firmer ground on the left. He who reaches Calf Crag with dry feet has cause to be satisfied with his boots.

Nab Crags and the Wyth Burn valley
(from the viewpoint indicated on the map above)

Waterfall in the Greenburn valley

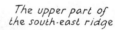
The upper part of
the south-east ridge

Tarn Crag

1801'

HIGH RAISE ▲ TARN CRAG ▲

SERGEANT MAN ▲

Grasmere ●

Dungeon Ghyll ●

MILES

0   1   2   3   4

from Easedale Tarn

NATURAL FEATURES

Ever since it first became fashionable to make excursions to behold the scenic wonders of the English Lake District Easedale Tarn has been a popular venue for visitors: a romantic setting, inurned in bracken-clad moraines with a background of craggy fells, and easy accessibility from Grasmere, have combined to make this a favourite place of resort. The dominant feature in the rugged skyline around the head of the tarn is the arching curve of Tarn Crag, above a wild rocky slope that plunges very steeply to the dark waters at its base. But rough though this slope is, it at least has the benefit of sunlight to colour and illuminate the grimness, whereas the opposite flanks, facing north into Far Easedale, form a scene of unrelieved gloom, with the black forbidding precipices of Deer Bields and Fern Gill seeming to cast a permanent shadow across the valley: one vertical and fissured crag here has quite a reputation amongst rock-climbers.

Easedale Tarn is not the only jewel in Tarn Crag's lap. A smaller sheet of water, Codale Tarn, occupies a hollow on a higher shelf; beyond, indefinite slopes climb to the top of the parent fell, High Raise.

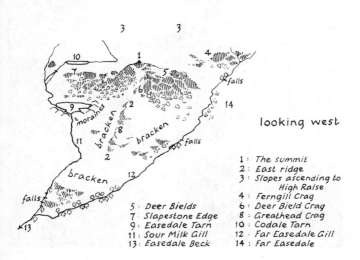

looking west

1 : The summit
2 : East ridge
3 : Slopes ascending to High Raise
4 : Ferngill Crag
5 : Deer Bields
6 : Deer Bield Crag
7 : Slapestone Edge
8 : Greathead Crag
9 : Easedale Tarn
10 : Codale Tarn
11 : Sour Milk Gill
12 : Far Easedale Gill
13 : Easedale Beck
14 : Far Easedale

Deer Bield Crag

MAP

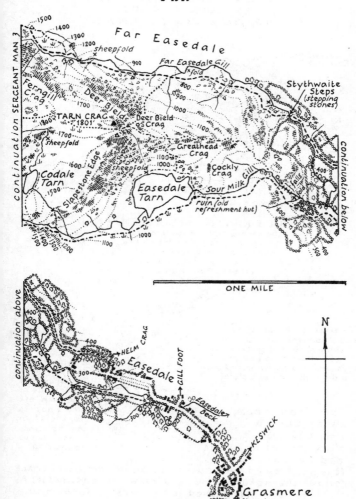

ONE MILE

N

ASCENT FROM GRASMERE
via SOUR MILK GILL
1600 feet of ascent : 3 miles

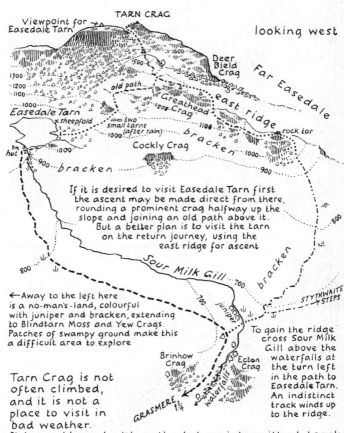

looking west

TARN CRAG

Viewpoint for Easedale Tarn

Deer Bield Crag

Far Easedale

east ridge

old path

Greathead Crag

Easedale Tarn

sheepfold

two small tarns (after rain)

rock tor

bracken

Cockly Crag

hut

bracken

bracken

If it is desired to visit Easedale Tarn first the ascent may be made direct from there, rounding a prominent crag halfway up the slope and joining an old path above it. But a better plan is to visit the tarn on the return journey, using the east ridge for ascent

Sour Milk Gill

juniper

STYTHWAITE STEPS

←Away to the left here is a no-man's-land, colourful with juniper and bracken, extending to Blindtarn Moss and Yew Crags. Patches of swampy ground make this a difficult area to explore

juniper

Brinhow Crag

Ecton Crag

waterfalls

To gain the ridge cross Sour Milk Gill above the waterfalls at the turn left in the path to Easedale Tarn. An indistinct track winds up to the ridge.

GRASMERE 1¼

Tarn Crag is not often climbed, and it is not a place to visit in bad weather.

It is not blessed with paths, but an intermittent track follows the natural line of ascent, the east ridge. As the summit is approached it assumes a formidable appearance but is easily reached by a grassy rake.

ASCENT FROM GRASMERE
via STYTHWAITE STEPS
1650 feet of ascent : 3½ miles

looking south-west

TARN CRAG

Viewpoint for Easedale Tarn

Easedale Tarn

old refreshment hut

Greathead Crag

east ridge

rock tor

Deer Bield Crag

The steep boulder slope above Deer Bield Crag may be avoided by a traverse left to the ridge.

Sour Milk Gill

juniper

east ridge

bracken

To gain the east ridge from Stythwaite Steps follow a poor track by the wall until Sour Milk Gill comes in sight, then turn up to the right.

fold & ruins

Stenners Crag

interesting boulders

Borrowdale path

sheepfold

Far Easedale Gill

Far Easedale

Stythwaite Steps (stepping stones)

GRASMERE 2

This approach to the east ridge is rather less attractive than that *via* Sour Milk Gill, but thereafter the route is the same. Walkers who want to see Deer Bield Crag at close quarters should continue along Far Easedale for nearly a mile beyond the stepping stones; the base of the Crag is reached from here by an easy slope.

THE SUMMIT

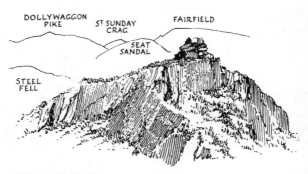

DOLLYWAGGON PIKE — St SUNDAY CRAG — FAIRFIELD — SEAT SANDAL — STEEL FELL

This is a beautiful little top, the highest point, a sharp peak, being just big enough to accommodate the neat cairn. Crags fall away steeply to east and south, but there are comfortable ledges from which the charming view of Grasmere may be surveyed in between searches for bilberries on the before-mentioned ledges which will probably prove fruitless. The broad summit of the fell is much broken by rocky outcrops and small tarns. The Ordnance Survey map is too generous with its 1800' contour, giving it a circumference of several hundred yards instead of a few feet, which is the maximum possible if in fact the highest point is 1801'.

DESCENTS : The only path on the fell (marked by cairns) traverses a grassy hollow 30 yards south of the cairn, and is the only way off. It goes down to the east ridge, for Grasmere. If it is desired to visit Easedale Tarn turn down to the right NOT at the foot of the first slope but 300 yards beyond at a grassy depression. From this depression Deer Bield Crag may be safely visited by turning left. Or it can be seen in profile merely by walking left 20 yards.

....

The summit crags

The cairn is reached, on grass, by rounding the pinnacle on the left

THE VIEW

Principal Fells

The outstanding feature is a splendid prospect of Easedale running down into the vale of Grasmere, a picture of great charm enhanced by the steep declivity in the foreground. The Helvellyn range is well seen, but there is little worthy of note in other directions.

Easedale Tarn cannot be seen from the main cairn although the hut there is in sight. Cross the grassy hollow to a big cairn 200 yards south and walk a few paces beyond for a striking bird's-eye view of the tarn.

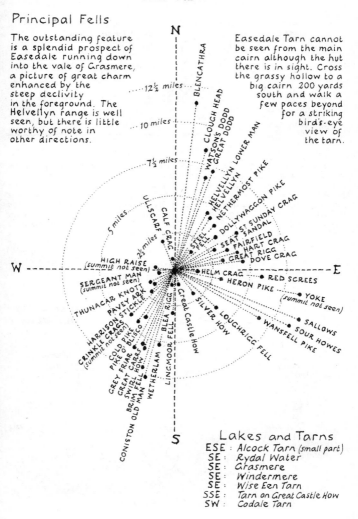

Lakes and Tarns

ESE : Alcock Tarn (small part)
SE : Rydal Water
SE : Grasmere
SE : Windermere
SE : Wise Een Tarn
SSE : Tarn on Great Castle How
SW : Codale Tarn

RIDGE ROUTE

To SERGEANT MAN, 2414' : 1¼ miles : W, then SW.
Slight depressions only : 700 feet of ascent
An interesting test in route-finding

There is no path. A continuous line of small cairns traces out an easy route across rough country, and is interesting to follow.   A grassy watercourse (distinctly seen from Tarn Crag) leads up to the boundary fence, but it is easier to turn left 100 yards short of the fence (after crossing a narrow tarn by stepping stones) and proceed south-west ; the abrupt peak of Sergeant Man soon comes in view for the first time during the walk.   Although there is nothing exciting about this route (there is little semblance of a ridge) the colourful slopes of heather, bilberry and mosses, intermingled with grey rocks, make it pleasant. *This walk is not recommended in mist: the cairns are too widely spaced to follow in poor visibility, and there are crags on all sides.*

Tarn Crag and its east ridge from Easedale

Sour Milk Gill

Sour Milk Gill

Thunacar Knott 2351'

from Harrison Stickle

From north and south and east and west, Thunacar Knott is completely unphotogenic, and the best that any illustration can produce is a slight roughness of the slowly-swelling curve that forms its broad summit. This uninspiring characteristic extends to the whole fell, which is quite deficient in interest (if, as has already been decided for the purposes of this book, Pavey Ark is not regarded as a part of it, although it really is). Grey stones on the summit and spilling in patches down the easy slopes to Langstrath, do little to relieve the drab monotony of spacious sheep-walks. When fixing the county boundaries between Cumberland and Westmorland the surveyors decided that the demarcation should make a sharp angle on the top — which is probably the most exciting thing that ever happened to Thunacar Knott.

The upper valley of Stake Beck, draining the western slopes in a dreary landscape of moraines, may yet bring a belated fame to the fell, for preliminary searches here suggest it as a likely area of activity by neolithic man.

HIGH RAISE
▲

THUNACAR ▲ KNOTT

HARRISON ▲ STICKLE

Old Hotel ● ● New Hotel
Dungeon Ghyll

MILES

0   1   2   3

MAP

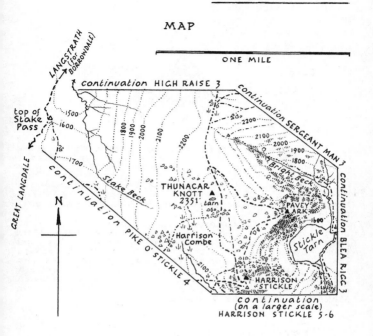

ONE MILE

LANGSTRATH (for BORROWDALE)

continuation HIGH RAISE 3

continuation SERGEANT MAN 3

top of Stake Pass

1500
1600

GREAT LANGDALE

1800 1900 2000 2100

2200

2100 2000 1900 1800

Bright Beck

continuation BLEA RIGG 3

1700

Stake Beck

continuation PIKE O' STICKLE 4

THUNACAR KNOTT 2351'

tarn

N

Harrison Combe

PAVEY ARK

1600

Stickle Tarn

2100

HARRISON STICKLE

continuation
(on a larger scale)
HARRISON STICKLE 5-6

ASCENT FROM DUNGEON GHYLL

Thunacar Knott is not popularly known by name, and is the one unattractive summit in a distinguished Langdale company. It is inconceivable, therefore, that anyone should set forth with the sole object of scaling this particular fell and no others en route, but such an eccentric person may exist, and must be provided with directions, although little space can be spared for notes that are not likely to be read. The direct ascent, if made at all, will be made from Dungeon Ghyll.

Refer to the diagrams of

path to THUNACAR KNOTT

N

line of cairns

2200

tor

2323

route

route

YARDS
0   100

HARRISON STICKLE

ascent for Harrison Stickle, and use Routes 1. 2 or 3, but beyond Thorn Crag and after starting the final rise to the top, watch for a line of small cairns rising to the left : these lead to a depression on the ridge north of the rock tor and here the ridge-path is met and may be traced, with a little difficulty at first, to Thunacar Knott

THE SUMMIT

The fell has two tops, with a tarn occupying the slight depression between. The recognised summit, surmounted by a well-made cairn, is a mound north of the tarn (which has interesting amphibious plant growth); the benchmark height is 2351'. A furlong south, however, the ground gradually rises to 2362' in an area of attractive grey stones. The ridge path crosses the higher top and passes 60 yards east of the main cairn.

DESCENTS : For Great Langdale, if it is not desired to visit the summit of Harrison Stickle en route, turn off the path thereto, following a line of cairns leading to the right from the depression between the two fells : this by-passes the Stickle, avoiding further climbing, and soon joins the regular path going down to Dungeon Ghyll. For Langstrath, the easy western slopes may be descended anywhere, with safety, in any sort of weather ; aim north of west, crossing Stake Beck to join the Stake Pass path.

The main summit from point 2362'
with High Raise beyond

RIDGE ROUTES

To HIGH RAISE, 2500': 1 mile : N
Depression at 2225': 275 feet of ascent
An easy walk, interesting only for the view

The path will be found 60 yards east of the cairn. It is not quite continuous, being lost for a short distance in marshy ground across the depression; otherwise it is distinct and direct, and mainly on grass. In mist, ignore branches turning off to the right.

To SERGEANT MAN, 2414':
1 mile : N, then E
Depression at 2225'
200 feet of ascent

An easy walk, with a good finish

Take the High Raise path, leaving it NOT at the first track going off to the right at the depression (this goes only to a cluster of grey rocks, amongst which is a good wind-shelter), but further, at a scatter of boulders, where alternative tracks branch off to the right, both being continuous to the dome-shaped top of Sergeant Man. This is strictly not a ridge walk but a skirting of the valley containing Bright Beck.

ONE MILE
(This is the scale of all three maps on this page)

N

To HARRISON STICKLE, 2403':
½ mile : S, then SSE
Depression at 2225'
150 feet of ascent

An easy walk, in improving scenery
Join the path 60 yards east of the cairn and follow it south, ascending slightly over point 2362', then down a grass slope before rising finally over rougher terrain to the top.

THE VIEW

Principal Fells

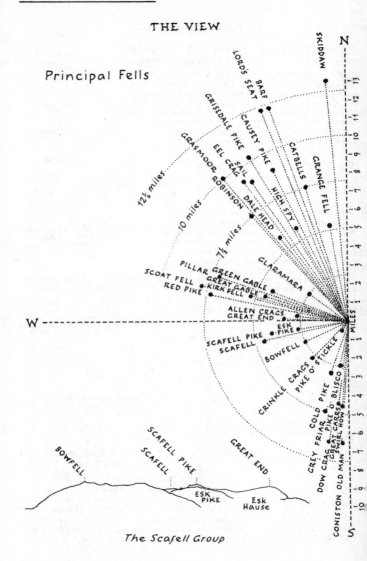

The Scafell Group

THE VIEW

This is the view from the main cairn, not from the slightly higher ground to the south. The scene is good westwards but disappointing eastwards, with an almost complete absence of water.

Lakes and Tarns

NNW: *Tarn at Leaves*
   (Rosthwaite Fell)
NNW: *Bassenthwaite Lake*
   (very small section)

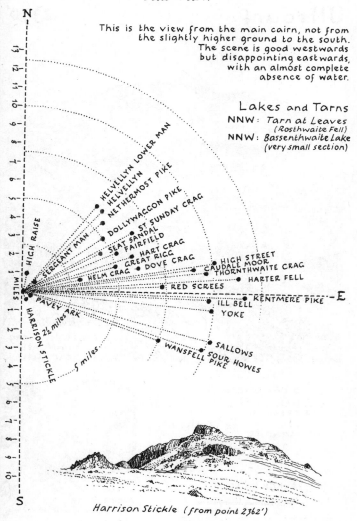

Harrison Stickle (from point 2362')

from Great Crag
Watendlath Fell

• Watendlath

• Rosthwaite
▲ GREAT CRAG

•   • Wythburn
Stonethwaite

▲ ULLSCARF

▲ HIGH RAISE

MILES
0   1   2   3   4

Binka Stone
near Dobgill Bridge

NATURAL FEATURES

Ullscarf rises from the surrounding valleys so steeply and with such a display of fierce crags that, up to 2,000 feet, it has all the makings of a great mountain. These crags defend the fell on most flanks, and there are few breaches in its seven-mile circumference of which walkers may take advantage to gain the summit without becoming involved in desperate scrambling. But unfortunately the higher slopes do not live up to the promise of the lower, being, in fact, quite featureless and inexpressibly dreary, with grass pastures swelling in easy gradients to the cairn marking the highest part of the summit plateau. Were it not for an old fence that crosses the top this would be a very bad place in mist for there are no natural landmarks to serve as guides and the wide and indefinite ridge changes direction repeatedly.

The crags are most in evidence above Thirlmere where they extend along the Wythburn valley and round into the wooded basin of Harrop Tarn, while others decorate the edge overlooking Greenup Gill. On the north side above Bleatarn Gill and near the Greenup pass they are absent and access is simple.

The main streams, Wyth Burn, Ullscarf Gill and Dob Gill, feed Thirlmere; Bleatarn Gill sets a course for Derwentwater, which it enters at Lodore; and a number of tributaries of Greenup Gill have carved ravines in the western face.

1: The summit
2: Ridge continuing to High Raise
3: Ridge continuing to Armboth Fell
4: Castle Crag
5: Nab Crags
6: Birk Crag
7: Tarn Crags
8: Standing Crag
9: Wyth Burn
10: Ullscarf Gill
11: Dob Gill
12: Harrop Tarn
13: Thirlmere
14: High Saddle
15: Low Saddle
16: Ridge continuing to Great Crag

looking west

Ullscarf 3

MAP

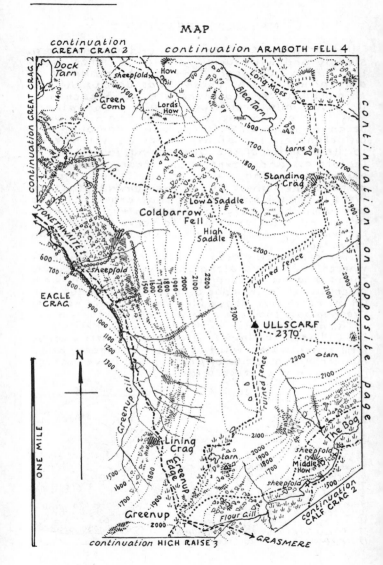

continuation on opposite page

Dock Tarn

How

Long Moss

Green Comb

Lords How

Blea Tarn

sheepfold

1500

1400

1600

1700

1800

tarns

1700

Standing Crag

STONETHWAITE

Low △ Saddle

Coldbarrow Fell

High Saddle

2200

ruined fence

1900

2000

600

700

800

sheepfold

1500
1600
1700
1800
1900
2000
2100
2200

2100

EAGLE CRAG

900

1000

2300

▲ ULLSCARF 2370'

1100

1200

1300

2200

tarn

2100

ruined fence

N

ONE MILE

Greenup Gill

2100

The Bog

Lining Crag

tarn

sheepfold

Greenup Edge

1500
1600
1700
1800
1900

2000
1900
1800
1700

Middle How

sheepfold

1500

Greenup

2000

Flour Gill

→ GRASMERE

MAP

Walkers on the Harrop Tarn-Watendlath route equipped with old maps should note that the course of the path over the ridge and across Long Moss has been changed slightly from the original in recent years.

Of the Lakeland fells over 2,000 feet Ullscarf will generally be adjudged the most central, and it is a pity that Nature has not endowed it with a distinctive superstructure worthy of the honour. If only the crags extended a thousand feet higher, and if only the summit took the shape of a Matterhorn! Instead of which, the top of the fell is the dullest imaginable. The most central, perhaps, but not, alas, a very distinguished pivot!

Ullscarf 5

The
*Wythburn
Valley*

a study
in
desolation

top
  The Bog

middle
  Wythburn Head Tarns

bottom
  the highest waterfall

ASCENT FROM WYTHBURN
1800 feet of ascent · 3½ miles (via West Head)

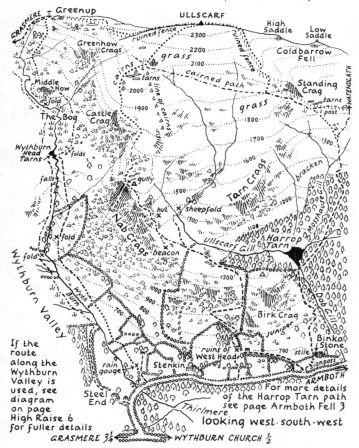

looking west-south-west

GRASMERE 3¼ ⟵⟶ WYTHBURN CHURCH ½

The middle route, from West Head Farm (demolished) and along the ridge overlooking the Wythburn valley, is the best in clear weather, but the ascent, although free from difficulty, should not be under-estimated: the upper slopes are pathless, unfrequented and vast, and route-selection is not too easy.

ASCENT FROM WATENDLATH
1600 feet of ascent : 3½ miles

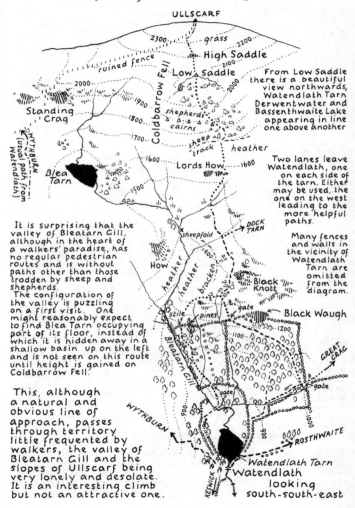

ULLSCARF

2300 — grass — 2200

High Saddle

ruined fence — Low Saddle

2000

Coldbarrow Fell

1900 — shepherds

Standing Crag

1800

cairns

1700

sheep track — heather

Blea Tarn

1600 — Lords How — 1600

1500

From Low Saddle there is a beautiful view northwards, Watendlath Tarn Derwentwater and Bassenthwaite Lake appearing in line one above another

Two lanes leave Watendlath, one on each side of the tarn. Either may be used, the one on the west leading to the more helpful paths.

Many fences and walls in the vicinity of Watendlath Tarn are omitted from the diagram.

sheepfold

DOCK TARN

How

heather — heather — 1400

heather — bracken

Black Knott

stile — pines

Black Waugh

1200

GREAT CRAG

Bleatarn Gill — 1100

gate

gate

900 — gate — 1000

WYTHBURN

ROSTHWAITE

WYTHBURN (usual path from Watendlath)

Watendlath Tarn

KESWICK — Watendlath looking south-south-east

It is surprising that the valley of Bleatarn Gill, although in the heart of a walkers' paradise, has no regular pedestrian routes and is without paths other than those trodden by sheep and shepherds.
The configuration of the valley is puzzling on a first visit. One might reasonably expect to find Blea Tarn occupying part of its floor, instead of which it is hidden away in a shallow basin up on the left and is not seen on this route until height is gained on Coldbarrow Fell.

This, although a natural and obvious line of approach, passes through territory little frequented by walkers, the valley of Bleatarn Gill and the slopes of Ullscarf being very lonely and desolate. It is an interesting climb but not an attractive one.

ASCENT FROM STONETHWAITE
2100 feet of ascent : 3¾ miles

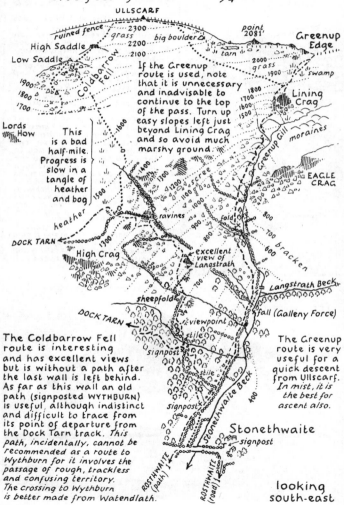

ULLSCARF

ruined fence — 2300
grass — 2200
High Saddle — 2100
Low Saddle
big boulder
point 2081'
Greenup Edge
tarn
2000 grass
1900 swamp

1900
1800
1700
Coldbarrow Fell
1600
1800
1700
1600
1500
Lining Crag

Lords How

This is a bad half-mile. Progress is slow in a tangle of heather and bog.

If the Greenup route is used, note that it is unnecessary and inadvisable to continue to the top of the pass. Turn up easy slopes left just beyond Lining Crag and so avoid much marshy ground.

Greenup Gill
moraines

1500
heather
1400
1300
1200
1100
1000
scree
ravines
900
800
fold
×
700
800
600
EAGLE CRAG

DOCK TARN
1300
High Crag
excellent view of Langstrath
700
bracken

Langstrath Beck
sheepfold
DOCK TARN
viewpoint
stile
fall (Galleny Force)
signpost
stile
signpost
Stonethwaite Beck
400
Stonethwaite
signpost

The Coldbarrow Fell route is interesting and has excellent views but is without a path after the last wall is left behind. As far as this wall an old path (signposted WYTHBURN) is useful, although indistinct and difficult to trace from its point of departure from the Dock Tarn track. *This path, incidentally, cannot be recommended as a route to Wythburn for it involves the passage of rough, trackless and confusing territory. The crossing to Wythburn is better made from Watendlath.*

The Greenup route is very useful for a quick descent from Ullscarf. In mist, it is the best for ascent also.

ROSTHWAITE (path)
ROSTHWAITE (road)

looking south-east

Lining Crag, Greenup

The Beacon, Nab Crags

But for the stupid conduct of a party of schoolboys, there would have been an illustration here of a fine beacon that stood on Nab Crags for half a century: it was a conspicuous landmark, a reliable guide for shepherds on the fells in bad weather, and it kept alive locally a memory of the Wythburn man who built it.

The boys (on holiday a few years ago from a school outside the district) wilfully destroyed the beacon and rolled the stones down the fellside. *Two masters were with the party during this senseless act of vandalism: two brainless idiots, a disgrace to their profession. Lakeland can do without visitors of this type.*

Malicious damage is beyond pardon, and a source of endless trouble to farmers and shepherds. Rolling or throwing stones down the fellsides is CRIMINAL —sheep have been killed and crippled by such reprehensible folly.

Respectable walkers (readers of this book, for example) should please stop mischief of this sort whenever they witness it —and punish the offenders to the best of their ability.

Standing Crag

THE SUMMIT

The top of Ullscarf is a cheerless
place, even in sunshine; in storm
there is no vestige of shelter. All
is grass on this vast summit, and
the only adornments are a cairn
and a line of forlorn fence posts
running both ways to the horizon;
the posts are now useless for the
purpose they originally served, but
for the lost wanderer they have a
real value in fixing his direction,
and they lead unerringly to the
highest point, which, without them,
would be in some doubt.

DESCENTS : Although the upper slopes are gently inclined,
and free from roughnesses, crags appear on all flanks when
the ground steepens and the absence of paths makes this a
particularly bad fell to get off in mist unless the safety of
the fence is preferred.

TO STONETHWAITE : Follow the fence south at first, but avoid the
marshy flats around point 2081' by bearing to the right well away
from the fence and joining the Greenup path above Lining Crag.

TO GRASMERE : Follow the fence south to Greenup Edge where the
path from Borrowdale will be joined.

TO WATENDLATH : There will be no difficulty in reversing the route
of ascent in clear weather, but in mist it is advisable to follow the
fence north beyond Standing Crag and join the cairned path from
Wythburn. Look for it near a big boulder on the left of the fence.

TO WYTHBURN (DIRECT) : This interesting way down calls for special
directions. There is no path until the sheepfold alongside Ullscarf Gill
is reached. From the summit proceed in the direction of Fairfield for
half a mile to a prominent rock tor with a cairn on top. Immediately
beyond is a maze of cairns which resolve into three distinct routes.
(These cairns, some of them very old, were erected by shepherds). A
fair path accompanies one line of cairns going left
(this traverses the fellside to the fence at Standing
Crag, and is of no help in the descent). The other
two lines of cairns are pathless and indicate only
the direction of safe descents. One leads down
directly towards Wythburn : when the cairns
end continue ahead and join Ullscarf Gill as
far as a big sheepfold at a meeting of becks,
where a path to West Head will be found on
the right bank. The other swings to the
right past some small tarns and goes
down to the grassy neck behind
Castle Crag where the ridge
may be followed to the West
Head path, or, alternatively,
a straight descent is possible
to Wythburn Head Tarns from
this point, leaving the ridge
with the crag on the left.

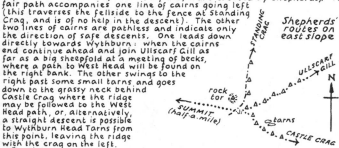

▌In mist, it is advisable to follow the fence north beyond Standing Crag
and join the path from Watendlath to Wythburn. The alternative, of
following the fence south to Greenup, thence descending the Wythburn
valley, takes much longer, while the valley itself is a bad place to be
in if the mist persists down at this level.

THE VIEW

Helvellyn's bulk hides most of the Far Eastern fells but otherwise the panorama is as comprehensive as one would expect from a fell right in the middle of things. It is a beautiful view, too, especially to west and north, although lacking somewhat in water content, Windermere being the only lake visible from the summit-cairn.

Principal Fells

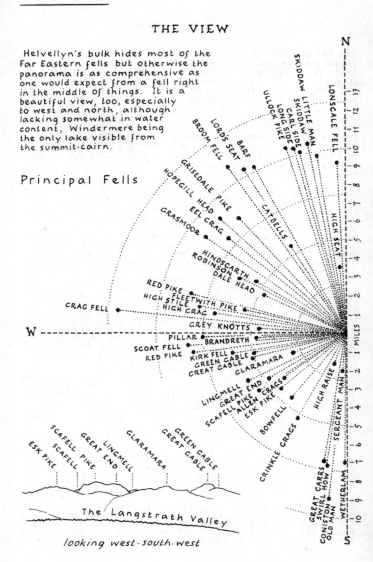

looking west-south-west

THE VIEW

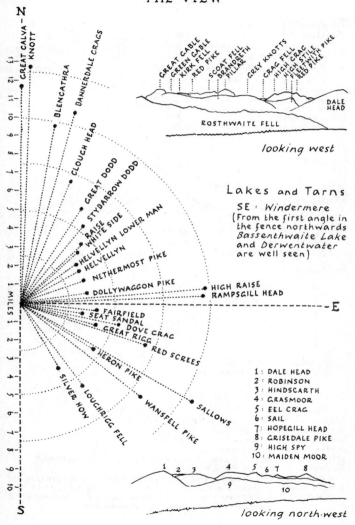

GREAT CALVA — KNOTT

BLENCATHRA

DANNERDALE CRAGS

CLOUGH HEAD

GREAT DODD

STYBARROW DODD

RAISE

WHITE SIDE

HELVELLYN LOWER MAN

HELVELLYN

NETHERMOST PIKE

DOLLYWAGGON PIKE

HIGH RAISE

RAMPSGILL HEAD

FAIRFIELD

SEAT SANDAL

DOVE CRAG

GREAT RIGG

RED SCREES

HERON PIKE

WANSFELL PIKE

SALLOWS

SILVER HOW

LOUGHRIGG FELL

N

S

1 MILES

E

GREAT GABLE
GREEN GABLE
KIRK FELL
RED PIKE
SCOAT FELL
BRANDRETH
PILLAR
GREY KNOTTS
CRAG FELL
HIGH CRAG
HIGH STILE
FLEETWITH PIKE
RED PIKE

DALE HEAD

ROSTHWAITE FELL

looking west

Lakes and Tarns

SE: *Windermere*
(From the first angle in
the fence northwards
Bassenthwaite Lake
and *Derwentwater*
are well seen)

1 : DALE HEAD
2 : ROBINSON
3 : HINDSCARTH
4 : GRASMOOR
5 : EEL CRAG
6 : SAIL
7 : HOPEGILL HEAD
8 : GRISEDALE PIKE
9 : HIGH SPY
10 : MAIDEN MOOR

looking north-west

RIDGE ROUTES

To ARMBOTH FELL, 1570': 3 miles
N, then NE, N, NW, N and NE
Sundry depressions, all marshy
250 feet of ascent
After rain, wear thigh-length gumboots
This is one of the wettest walks
in Lakeland, and not one to
be undertaken for pleasure.
Make use of the diagram,
if interested; ordinary
words are inadequate.

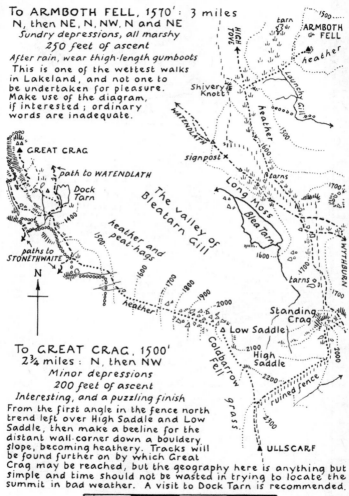

To GREAT CRAG, 1500'
2¾ miles: N, then NW
Minor depressions
200 feet of ascent
Interesting, and a puzzling finish
From the first angle in the fence north
trend left over High Saddle and Low
Saddle, then make a beeline for the
distant wall-corner down a bouldery
slope, becoming heathery. Tracks will
be found further on by which Great
Crag may be reached, but the geography here is anything but
simple and time should not be wasted in trying to locate the
summit in bad weather. A visit to Dock Tarn is recommended.

ONE MILE

RIDGE ROUTE

To HIGH RAISE, 2500' : 2¼ miles
S, then SW, S and SW
Depression at 1995'
520 feet of ascent
A tedious walk, safe in mist

The only direction necessary is to follow
the old fence, some small detours being
advisable to avoid swampy ground.
 Good views are some compensation
for the dullness of the immediate
surroundings, but there are many
better walks in Lakeland than this!

looking south·west
 1 : HIGH RAISE
 2 : CRINKLE CRAGS
 3 : BOWFELL

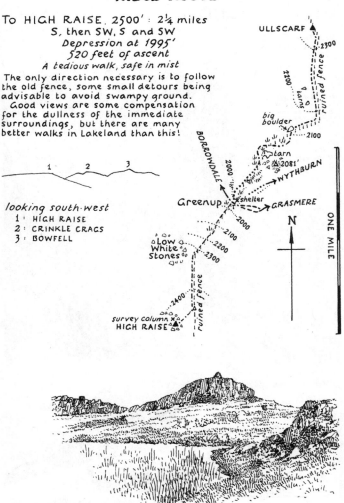

The tarn and point 2081'

Walla Crag

'Wallow Crag'
on old editions
of Ordnance
Survey maps

*Some walkers have
difficulty in
remembering
the altitudes
of the fells.
There is no
excuse here
for anybody
who can
count up
to four.*

from Falcon Crag

• Keswick
  • Rakefoot
  ▲ WALLA CRAG
  BLEABERRY
  ▲ FELL
• Lodore

MILES
0   1   2   3

from near Rakefoot

NATURAL FEATURES

The pleasant Vale of Keswick, surely one of earth's sweetest landscapes, is surrounded by mountains of noble proportions with an inner circle of lesser fells which deserve more than the name of foothills, each having strong individual characteristics, a definite and distinctive appearance, and a natural beauty all its own. Among these is Walla Crag, an eminence of intermingled rocks and trees overlooking the east shore of lovely Derwentwater: of moderate elevation yet steep, romantic, challenging. Seen from the lake the hoary top seems unattainable, yet it may be gained by the gentlest of ascents for the slopes beyond the upper fringe of crag descend easily, accompanied by Brockle Beck, almost to the streets of Keswick.

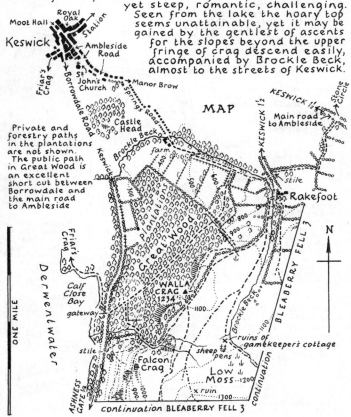

MAP

Private and forestry paths in the plantations are not shown. The public path in Great Wood is an excellent short cut between Borrowdale and the main road to Ambleside

ONE MILE

ASCENT FROM KESWICK
1000 feet of ascent : 2½ miles

On a first visit it is easy to go astray here. The good cart-track from Rakefoot continues (soon deteriorating) in the direction of Bleaberry Fell: the less distinct branch path to Walla Crag follows the wall round to the right. Parties have been found toiling up Bleaberry Fell under the impression that they were climbing Walla Crag, an excusable mistake, for the former comes clearly into view ahead from the cart-track while the latter is out of sight, and, in any case, is not conspicuous from this side. A signpost would be useful at this point.

Note that an exciting (but unofficial) path passes through this gap in the wall and skirts the edge of the escarpment on its way to the summit, providing excellent views en route.

The iron grid in the cart-track was installed by the Army to facilitate the passage of tanks during the war, when the fell was a training ground.

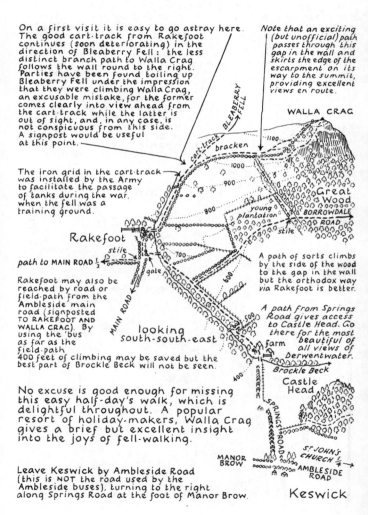

Rakefoot

path to MAIN ROAD ½

Rakefoot may also be reached by road or field-path from the Ambleside main road (signposted TO RAKEFOOT and WALLA CRAG). By using the 'bus as far as the field-path 400 feet of climbing may be saved but the best part of Brockle Beck will not be seen.

looking south-south-east

A path of sorts climbs by the side of the wood to the gap in the wall but the orthodox way via Rakefoot is better.

A path from Springs Road gives access to Castle Head. Go there for the most beautiful of all views of Derwentwater.

No excuse is good enough for missing this easy half-day's walk, which is delightful throughout. A popular resort of holiday-makers, Walla Crag gives a brief but excellent insight into the joys of fell-walking.

Leave Keswick by Ambleside Road (this is NOT the road used by the Ambleside buses), turning to the right along Springs Road at the foot of Manor Brow.

Keswick

ASCENT FROM THE BORROWDALE ROAD
950 feet of ascent : 1 mile (2½ from Keswick)

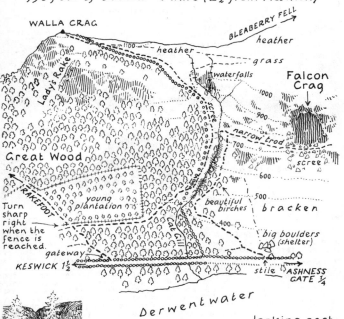

WALLA CRAG

BLEABERRY FELL

heather

heather

grass

1100

waterfalls

Falcon Crag

Lady's Rake

1000

900

narrow trod

700

Great Wood

scree

600

RAKEFOOT

young plantation

500

beautiful birches

bracken

Turn sharp right when the fence is reached.

400

big boulders (shelter)

gateway

KESWICK 1½

stile   ASHNESS GATE ¼

Derwentwater

looking east

Alternative starts are given. The 'purest' route is that from the gateway, which keeps throughout to the Walla Crag side of Cat Gill, but trees shut out views that are too good to be missed. This defect is remedied by starting from the stile 150 yards beyond the point where the road crosses Cat Gill, a route with excellent views but calling for a little care higher up, just before joining the other path on the north bank of the gill. (A narrow trod here, on the south bank, leads excitingly to the base of Falcon Crag, which is worth seeing at close quarters, especially so from the small rise beyond).

A beautiful short climb up steep colourful slopes overlooking Derwentwater. If the starting point on the road is reached via Friar's Crag and Calf Close Bay, and if the return is made via Rakefoot and Brockle Beck, this becomes the best walk easily attainable in a half-day from Keswick.

Waterfalls in Cat Gill

THE SUMMIT

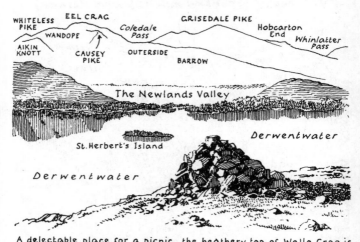

WHITELESS PIKE · EEL CRAG · Coledale Pass · GRISEDALE PIKE · Hobcarton End · Whinlatter Pass

AIKIN KNOTT · WANDOPE · CAUSEY PIKE · OUTERSIDE · BARROW

The Newlands Valley

St. Herbert's Island · Derwentwater

Derwentwater

A delectable place for a picnic, the heathery top of Walla Crag is also a favourite viewpoint for Derwentwater, seen directly below the long steep escarpment. A profusion of decayed tree-stumps indicates that the summit, now bare, was at one time thickly wooded; many trees survive nearby, all west of the wall crossing the top of the fell, as is the cairn, 60 yards distant.

DESCENTS: Keep to the paths: the dangers of straying from them should be obvious. An inviting opening in the cliff (Lady's Rake) 150 yards south of the cairn is a trap to be avoided. In mist, note that the wall links Rakefoot and the Borrowdale road, and that the paths follow it. The descent to Rakefoot is easy; the other route is rough but more interesting.

RIDGE ROUTE

TO BLEABERRY FELL, 1932'
1¼ miles : S, then SSE curving SE
Depression at 1070'
900 feet of ascent

A dull climb relieved by fine views

Start along the Ashness Bridge path, crossing to a higher track when a stream is reached and then aiming for the left side of the prominent mound. Detour right to join the first cairn.

THE VIEW

This well-known view has earned its popularity not by its extensiveness but by the variety and charm of many nearby features, with Borrowdale an outstanding study of mountain grouping and the exciting downward prospect of Derwentwater of more general appeal. An interesting emphasis is placed on the relatively low elevation of much of the central part of Lakeland by the distant view of Grey Friar in the Coniston fells — hardly to be expected from Walla Crag's modest height so far to the north.

Principal Fells

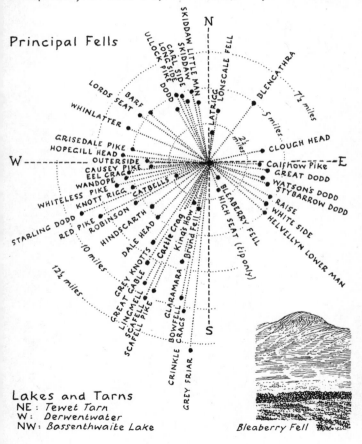

N

SKIDDAW LITTLE MAN
SKIDDAW
CARL SIDE
LONG SIDE
ULLOCK PIKE
DODD
LORDS SEAT
BARF
WHINLATTER
LONSCALE FELL
LATRIGG
BLENCATHRA
7½ miles
GRISEDALE PIKE
HOPEGILL HEAD
OUTSIDE
CAUSEY PIKE
EEL CRAG
WANDOPE
WHITELESS PIKE
KNOTT RIGG
CATBELLS
STARLING DODD
RED PIKE
ROBINSON
HINDSCARTH
DALE HEAD
GREY KNOTTS
GREAT GABLE
LINGMELL
SCAFELL
SCAFELL PIKE
CRINKLE CRAGS
BOWFELL
GLARAMARA
Castle Crag
King's How
Brund Fell
BLEABERRY FELL
HIGH SEAT (tip only)
CLOUGH HEAD
Calfhow Pike
GREAT DODD
WATSON'S DODD
STYBARROW DODD
RAISE
WHITE SIDE
HELVELLYN LOWER MAN
5 miles
2½ miles
10 miles
12½ miles
GREY FRIAR

W — — — — — E

S

Lakes and Tarns
NE: Tewet Tarn
W: Derwentwater
NW: Bassenthwaite Lake

Bleaberry Fell

THE CENTRAL FELLS

Some Personal notes
in conclusion

If I were thirty years younger I should already be looking forward to the time when, with the seventh and last book in this series finished (round about 1965) I could start to go over all the ground once again with a view to making such revisions as may be found to be necessary. I fear, however, that by that time age will have shackled my limbs to such an extent that the joyful task may be beyond me.

Guidebooks that are inaccurate and unreliable are worse than none at all, and I am aware that in a few small respects Books One and Two are already out of date. It is most exasperating, for instance, to learn of fences appearing on land where I have shown none, or of the erection of new buildings, or that signposts or cairns have been destroyed or established — all in the short interval since the books were originally published. Even as I write, there is a proposal afoot to demolish the dam at Stickle Tarn, which would shrink considerably the size of the tarn, and alter its shape — and this news comes to me only a few days after sending to the printer several pages which feature the tarn and on which its present proportions are most carefully delineated. There is no stopping these changes — but I do wish people would leave things alone! Substantially, of course, the books will be useful for many years to come, especially in the detail and description of the fell tops, while the views will remain unaltered for ever, assuming that falling satellites and other fancy gadgets of man's invention don't blow God's far worthier creations to bits. But, this dire possibility apart, the books must inevitably show more and more inaccuracies as the years go by. Therefore, because it is unlikely that there will ever be revised editions, and because I should just hate to see my name on anything that could not be relied on, the probability is that the books will progressively be withdrawn from publication after a currency of a few years.

All this is leading to a suggestion that readers who are really enthusiastic about fellwalking and have several more seasons of happy wandering to look forward to, should start to use these volumes as basic notebooks for their own personal records, making such amendments (neatly, I hope!) as they find necessary during their walks and adapting the page-margins for dates and details of their own ascents and other notes of special interest.

I had intended (under pressure from publisher, printer and booksellers alike) to demonstrate in these final pages that an increase in the price of the books had become urgently necessary to cover rising costs of production — but I haven't left myself enough space to do it; besides, I have no stomach for such unpalatable discourse. So for the time being the price will continue uniform at 12s 6d — let's say for the sake of tidiness.

Away with such trivial matters! It is better by far that my last few lines should tell of the Central Fells, even though this area will already be well known to most readers and in places is much frequented; indeed the presence of other walkers was often rather an embarrassment to me, although my mission was never suspected. The popular heights above Derwentwater I left until the holiday crowds (and Vivian Fisher, _and_ his gate!) had all departed from the scene. Alone, what a celestial beauty I found there in the quiet of late autumn and early winter! What rich warm colour! I walked on golden carpets between golden tapestries, marvelling anew at the supreme craftsmanship that had created so great a loveliness, and at my own good fortune to be in its midst, enjoying a heaven I had done nothing to deserve. One cannot find the words to describe it: only an inexpressible humility fills the heart....

12s 6d, 15s, 17s 6d — what does it matter? I must hasten now to the Scafells, noblest of Lakeland's cathedrals, while good health and appreciation of beauty and simple reverence and gratitude remain with me, for when I have lost these blessings I shall have little left. This one lesson, above all others, the hills have taught me.

new year 1958   AW.